WHITLEY STRIEBER'S HIDDEN AGENDAS

Whitley Strieber brings to
WHITLEY STRIEBER'S
most respected names in
Strieber gathers together
controversial issues as con
ters, and other unexplained phenomena. Drawing on his vast
knowledge and experience, spanning the globe and exploring
a wide variety of subjects, Strieber brings us unprecedented
access to information from reliable sources—revelations that
will rock our deepest beliefs and may open a door to worlds
other than our own.

FROM THE INNER WORLD OF THE
FATIMA APPARITIONS TO THE HIDDEN
RECESSES OF THE VATICAN,
DISCOVER THE TRUTH . . .

* How The Virgin Mary, acting through Pope John Paul II,
helped to bring down Polish Communism and affect
the collapse of the USSR.

*Why Marian apparitions and UFO warnings seem to be
telling us we are at a critical turning point in human
evolution. To ignore them invites disaster.

* Why the awesome "dance of the sun," witnessed first
at Fatima on October 13, 1917, and
again throughout the century, is a message
from another world.

Follow the miracles and learn . . .

THE FATIMA SECRET

THE FATIMA SECRET

MICHAEL HESEMANN

A DELL BOOK

Published by
Dell Publishing
a division of
Random House, Inc.
1540 Broadway
New York, New York 10036

Dell books may be purchased for business or promotional use or for special sales. For information please write to: Special Markets Department, Random House, Inc., 1540 Broadway, New York, N.Y. 10036.

ISBN: 0-440-23644-4

Printed in the United States of America

Published simultaneously in Canada

December 2000

10 9 8 7 6 5 4 3 2 1

OPM

THE
FATIMA
SECRET

INTRODUCTION
by WHITLEY STRIEBER

IN THE SUMMER of 1917, during the height of World War I, three small children in the obscure village of Fatima in neutral Portugal began to report that they were seeing a "beautiful lady" who was coming to them out of the sky. The lady delivered three secrets. When, in 1960, Pope John XXIII opened the Third Secret, some of those closest to him reported that he almost fainted with horror.

This book, written by a man close to many Vatican insiders, represents an informed attempt to discover what it was that so horrified John XXIII, and that has been kept secret by every pope who has followed.

The First Secret was a terrifying vision of hell, revealed at the time of the apparitions. It was certainly sobering, but not really prophetic in nature, except perhaps to those who might be destined to taste the fire.

The second was quite extraordinary: "This war is going to end. But if they do not stop offending God, another and worse war will break out. . . . When you see a night illuminated by an unknown light, know that God . . . is going to punish the world for its crimes by means of war, hunger, and persecution of the Church."

The secret was revealed in 1928, and it can be argued that its specific reference to the fact that World War I would end could have been added later, since the secret was not made public until long after the war was over.

The phrase *when you see a night illuminated by an unknown light* was definitively recorded as part of the secret when it was originally revealed. In January of 1938, ten years later, an extraordinary light was indeed observed both by astronomers and the public throughout western Europe. This highly unusual auroral effect lasted for two hours, and created such brightness in many areas that it was like moonlight.

In March of 1938 Germany annexed the Sudetenland from Czechoslovakia, effectively beginning World War II.

Obviously, the advent of the light and the subsequent beginning of the war could not have been known in 1928. And yet, the prophecy is there.

The question is, does it matter? Are Marian apparitions simple hallucinations, or something more mysterious? And if they are more extraordinary, then how should we approach them?

When one looks at the evidence, an unexpectedly compelling—and very strange—picture emerges.

My own interest in Marian apparitions was kindled indirectly, by a meeting with a remarkable man who was an expert on the Shroud of Turin. It was during the early seventies that I met Father Peter Rinaldi, who was in New York trying to get contributions for what then seemed like a truly quixotic quest: he wanted to help two air force scientists, Drs. Eric Jumper and John Jackson, to expose the Shroud of Turin to scientific study. They felt that the use of modern scientific techniques such as carbon dating could determine whether or not it was authentically from the era during which Jesus had lived.

He gave such a fascinating, even inspiring, presentation on the shroud that I found that my checkbook had come into my hands almost on its own. In the course of our brief relationship Father Rinaldi told me a story about Fatima. He knew a priest who had actually been there, and this priest had personally witnessed the miracle of Fatima.

The miracle, which will be discussed extensively in this book, began on September 13, 1917. Prior to that date the recurring apparition had been witnessed only by three children. At that time there were about twenty-five thousand people at the Cova da Íria, the site near Fatima of what had become a highly controversial series of apparitions being claimed by three village children. On that day Monsignor John Quaresma reported that "I saw, clearly and distinctly, a luminous globe, which moved from the east to the west, gliding slowly and majestically through space."

This object was seen by thousands of people, and led to a massive crowd on the next appointed day of the apparition, a month later on October 13. This time, upward of seventy thousand people were present, including Father Rinaldi's friend. This was the day of the greatest of the Fatima miracles. The sun changed its appearance completely, becoming a dull copper color and seeming to move about in the sky. Father Rinaldi told me that his friend, who had been some distance from the Cova da Íria due to the crowds, nevertheless saw something quite amazing. "It was not the sun. He said that it was a huge disk that moved in front of the sun. He could make out some sort of activity taking place on its surface, as if somebody was moving there."

Any modern individual would say that this appeared more like a UFO sighting than a Marian apparition. There are even those who would turn it upside down, and say that it was demonic deceit. However, this would ignore the deep and profound relationship between the modern UFO phenomenon and the apparitional miracles of the past. In his book *Passport to Magonia* legendary UFO investigator Jacques Vallée offered a history of apparitions, ranging from the appearance of sylphs, the small forest deities of the Greeks and Romans, to the wee folk of the medieval fairy faith, ending with modern Marian apparitions and visions of UFO occupants.

However, there is a substantial difference between Marian apparitions and the others. Neither modern close-encounter lore nor the ancient fairy faith, which reports encounters with beings that are strikingly similar to contemporary UFO occupants, can approach the Marian material in this one crucial way. UFO occupants, like the fairy folk before them, have, at best, a localized and tangential effect on the social order.

While this in no way is meant to suggest any particular origin for any of the apparitions and visitations, it is important to understand that the Marian material is the most socially potent by far. Marian apparitions are unique in that they have received such a powerful response that they have often led to identifiable historical change.

Fatima is not the only example of this. Another is the apparition of Our Lady of Guadalupe in Mexico in 1531. This was a powerful event that unfolded at an extremely high level of strangeness. What made it so strange was the way in which it reduced conflict between Spanish Catholicism and native Mexican religions. It is scarcely possible that anybody in that era would have had the sociological knowledge necessary to have done this. And yet it happened.

At the time the conquered Mexican Indians were not even considered fully human by the Spaniards. It was no sin to enslave them, no crime to murder them. Their ancient culture had been swept aside over the course of a brief conquest, and they were being slaughtered by their conquerors and decimated by disease. The native people of Mexico were headed for extinction.

An Aztec, Juan Diego, was one of the few Indians who had converted to Catholicism. He and his wife had been baptized at the Church of Santiago, built in the rubble of the temple of Huitzilpochtli, which had been razed by the Spaniards shortly after the conquest. In the early morning hours of December 9 he had left mass and was passing Tepeyac hill on his way to a class run by the Franciscans. As he went around the hill, he heard singing. He stopped. This hill was a sacred Aztec site, which he would certainly have known. In fact, it was sacred to the rain goddess, one of the most important of all deities in this dry country. He next heard a voice, and ran up the hill. There he confronted the apparition of a magnificent celestial being, a woman clothed in light. What appeared to him to be a Catholic saint stood on a site sacred to a goddess from the older culture, thus forming a bridge between two worlds that were at that time in profound conflict. Powerful economic forces in New Spain preferred to view the Indians as subhuman so that they could be used and controlled more easily. The Church, to some degree, stood against this, but not even all churchmen were in agreement that the Indians deserved the treatment due human beings.

Juan Diego reported that the woman described herself to him as the Mother of God and asked that a temple be built on the site. He was told to go to the bishop and repeat this request.

It was important that the bishop was a Franciscan, because this order was resisting attempts to enslave the Indians. However, the bishop did not believe Juan Diego's peculiar story. At this time apparitions of the Virgin were extremely uncommon, and far from being a part of the culture of Catholicism that they have since become.

As he had been asked, he returned to the hill, where the apparition was patiently waiting for news about her request. He was told to go back to the bishop and ask again. The bishop, hearing the story a second time, was moved by Juan Diego's passion and determination. However, he had no history to guide him, and no concept of how to react to the very new notion that the Virgin might actually appear to people and attempt to communicate with them. He asked for a sign from her, and also sent people to follow Juan Diego.

When Diego seemed to his followers to elude them, they returned to the bishop and suggested that he was lying. Later, he went to the top of the hill where the Lady had appeared and was mystified to find that it was now covered with flowers. She told him to pick the flowers and take them to the bishop.

He did so, only to find that the residence was now guarded. The servants who had lost him now came out and began to accuse him of lying. When they realized that he was carrying something in his *tilma,* they demanded to see what it was. He tried to hide its contents from them, but finally let them glimpse the roses. Such flowers did not bloom in December, so they told the bishop that Juan Diego did indeed have a sign from the Lady and the bishop received him. When Juan Diego opened the *tilma,* everybody was shocked to see a painting of the Lady slowly materialize on the roughly woven cloth.

This was taken as a powerful sign, and the Virgin of Guadalupe became the patron saint of Mexico. Because the sign had been given to an Indian, the forces that wanted to enslave them lost their political strength, and the Spaniards were compelled by the Church to recognize them as human beings. While their treatment improved only slowly, their basic human rights were grudgingly recognized by their conquerors. At the same time, the message of the Lady changed the attitude of the Indians toward Christianity. Because they saw her as their rescuer and a powerful miracle worker, their previous hostility was transformed, and thousands of them began converting. Over the course of the next decade millions of Indians—in fact, almost the entire native population of Mexico—converted.

For the past 450 years, as reverence for the Virgin of Guadalupe and the memories of the old gods have combined to create a uniquely Mexican Catholicism, many dozens of skeptics have stepped forward and made efforts to prove that the painting on the *tilma* has an ordinary origin. This garment is made of cactus cloth, woven of strands pulled from the stringy body of certain varieties of cactus and made into a rough thread. The *tilma* remains intact after 450 years, despite its being made of this fragile organic substance. Infrared photography, ultraviolet photography, and computer-enhanced black-

and-white photography have been used to study the painting.

What has been determined is that there is no under-sketch—that is to say, the painting was made on the un-marked cloth. The artist did not first prepare his work area by sketching an outline on it of what he would paint. Had it been made by a human artist, an undersketch would have almost certainly been present, as is true of al-most all other works of similar complexity and artistry. In addition, while the portrait does appear to be painted, it has not been possible to determine which pigments and dyes were used. In addition to the strange state of preser-vation of the unsized cactus cloth, the paints themselves have not cracked or faded in 450 years. For the first 250 years of its life the painting was kept in an open frame, unprotected from candle smoke, incense, and human touch. In tests done on the *tilma* it has been determined that it was in no way prepared to receive the paint. Nev-ertheless, the paint lies only upon the surface of the cloth. There is no seepage through to the back.

Oddly, twentieth-century photographic analysis has revealed that the image contains in its eyes what appears to be the reflection of its surroundings at the time that it was made. There are four human images present, possi-bly Juan Diego, the bishop and his interpreter, and a fourth person, believed to be a woman. In addition, the image has been created entirely without detectable brushstrokes.

Like the Shroud of Turin, which bears a mysteriously

deposited image of a man bearing the wounds of Christ's passion, the Image of Guadalupe has become more mysterious as science has become more sophisticated. Carbon dating, for example, placed the origin of the shroud in the twelfth century A.D., over a thousand years after Christ's passion. But more sophisticated techniques have not only revised the date to the second century A.D. or before, but revealed that the cloth was present for some years in the immediate area of Jerusalem. This has been accomplished by revising the carbon dating data to reflect the presence of residue from a fifteenth-century fire that scorched it, and for the presence of bacteria on the surface that was left by handling. The shroud has been determined to have spent time in the immediate area of Jerusalem by the presence on it of the pollens of plants that are known only in that region.

The apparition at Guadalupe was spectacularly powerful, with a few bold strokes completely redefining a whole culture and forever altering the nature of human relationships within it.

Since Guadalupe, Marian apparitions have become more frequent. The visions have appealed for churches to be built, offered moral advice and warnings, expressed direct concern about Communism, and even promised and apparently sent a sign warning of the imminent outbreak of World War II. This sign, which is discussed in this book, is itself a powerful mystery and again suggests that there may indeed be a higher power taking an interest in human affairs.

The appearance of lights in connection with the Virgin, and especially the events at Fatima, have prompted many UFO researchers to speculate that there may be a relationship between UFOs and Marian apparitions. The parallels between some of the phenomena observed during Marian apparitions and UFOs are obvious and the author does not deny that. Still, he has tried to avoid any interpretation, preferring to tell the history of the Fatima events in their own light.

The reason why Michael Hesemann prefers to let the readers find these correlations by themselves is to avoid premature speculation. In the past several UFO researchers, prominently Jacques Vallée, have pointed to these parallels. Others have used them to argue that Marian apparitions are caused by extraterrestrial intelligences. Hesemann, although considered one of Europe's leading experts on the UFO phenomenon, rather points to the dangers of generalization. "You can't explain one phenomenon you don't understand by another phenomenon you understand even less," he has said.

He also points to the fact that the Marian messages have included "precise and completely fulfilled predictions, both about the future of mankind and the personal fate of the visionaries." The deep and powerful cultural changes that have sometimes come about as a result of Marian apparitions, such as that of Our Lady of Guadalupe, would appear to be seated in the cultural and social realities of human life. One would think that an approach by aliens would be less sensitive to the hidden structures of human society, and less able to so precisely effect change.

However, if there has been an extraterrestrial presence here for a long time, it seems inevitable that it would be profoundly involved in human society, and possibly in just the indirect and yet deeply insightful and influential manner displayed by the Marian apparitions.

Within Catholicism there is an effort presently being made to redefine our concept of God in such a way that it more accurately reflects the immensity and complexity of the universe around us. It is within the context of such an effort that we might hope to address mysteries like the Marian apparitions with more accuracy than we can at present.

At the annual congress of the American Association for the Advancement of Science, when the implications of the possible discovery of remains of bacterial life in a meteorite from Mars were discussed, Dr. Christopher Corbally of the Vatican Observatory in Tucson, Arizona, said, "We only have to extend the concept of an 'anthropocentric God' toward a God which is more almighty than we were ever able to imagine." The discovery that we are not alone in the universe would reveal to mankind that "we are an integral part of a cosmic community. We would discover a Church which goes far beyond the limits of the Earth and any narrow interpretation of the Bible and other scriptures."

Several UFO researchers are convinced that indeed there is a connection between the UFO phenomenon and

Marian apparitions. In 1962 the French author Paul Misraki ("Paul Thomas"), in his book *Les Extraterrestres,* suggested parallels between the "miracle of the sun" in Fatima and modern UFO appearances. Others followed, such as Spanish researcher Antonio Ribera, who believed all events in Fatima were just "misinterpreted extraterrestrial encounters" (Ribera 1964), or French researcher Jacques Vallée, who in his book *The Invisible College* (1975) published the most comprehensive study on parallels between Fatima and UFO encounters.

Additionally, witnesses confirmed activities in the skies in connection with the Fatima events. For example the parish priest of Fatima stated that "on this 13th [of September 1917] at about 3:00 P.M. the Reverend Antonio de Figueiredo, who is a highly respected Professor at the seminary in Santarém, came to our house and stated that he saw stars in a lower sphere/region than their usual sphere/region and that he came to me for the sole reason of informing me about this."

Today, such a sighting would be considered a UFO event.

After a six-year study of Fatima, Joachim Fernandes and Dr. Dina d'Armada of the Portuguese National Investigation Committee for the UFO Phenomenon (CNIFO) came to the conclusion: "The documents confirm that the female being [the Madonna] was transported in a tronco-conical light beam which gradually expanded, being either emitted or returning to a source, and that this source most probably was within a 'cloud' which made unusual and special movements, e.g., contrary to the wind. There are modern examples for this phenomenon, called 'solid light.' " (They refer here to laser light, which was in an early experimental state at the time, and the term *tronco-conical* is an attempt to describe the shape of the beam of light, which appeared like a cone.)

Are Marian apparitions, then, light projections of some sort caused by an unknown intelligence that is using our own beliefs to gain authority for its advice and suggestions?

Howard Menger, one of the controversial "contactees" of the 1950s, claimed that he, as a young boy in 1941, encountered a "beautiful Lady" in rural High Bridge, New Jersey, where his parents had a farm. "I have come a long way to see you and to talk with you," she told him. She promised to return and did so in 1946. Menger wrote in his book *From Outer Space to You:*

At that moment there was a tremendous flash of light and the sense of heat in the back of my neck. I turned. Above the vast western section of the field a huge fireball moved at tremendous speed.... The ball of fire looked like a huge spinning sun, shining, pulsating, and changing colors. It hovered over the field, as I stood watching it, seemingly transfixed. The pulsating color changes diminished and the fireball turned into a metallic-looking craft, surrounded by portholes. ... Soon an opening appeared on a

flange around the bottom of the craft. . . . Through
the large opening in the craft stepped a beautiful
woman. She had long blond hair and was dressed in
(an) . . . outfit which fitted loosely over what was a
shapely body. The material was semitranslucent, of
a soft pastel color which seemed to glow.

Menger is aware of the mystic nature of his experiences and believes he encountered angels. He does not
associate this experience with Mary, but somebody from
the Catholic religious tradition might, and indeed, there
is nothing to say that he did not encounter the same phenomenon that was observed by thousands at Fatima.

Angels in Starships is the title of a book written by
Italian contactee Giorgio Dibitonto. Dibitonto claims
that he was led to a remote valley by an angel on April
23, 1980, when in front of him a white, bell-shaped disk
landed from which he heard a voice saying:

"This is not the first time that we encounter humans in
this way. Since ancient times we spoke to your mankind
from our starships. In your Holy Scripture you read that
the Lord spoke to the men on Earth from a cloud and
what you are experiencing now for the first time is the
same as your fathers experienced in ancient times . . . we
come from the many mansions of the father. . . ."

The voice identified itself as an angel named
Raphael. He went on to say that earth had once been a
Garden of Eden where man lived in harmony with the
laws of creation. But mankind, in deciding to go down

"the poor paths of evil," departed from the cosmic order. "We are the cherubim of the Scripture, the Watchers of Eden. Never will we allow mankind to enter the immaculate space as long as you do not convert from creatures of evil to creatures of universal love."

Dibitonto had further contacts in which he received several warnings and teachings, all regarding the threat of human self-destruction. And eventually he learned about the Mother of God: "The mother in the flesh of Jesus is, after the Lord Himself, the wisest, most gracious heavenly being. Her love for the Father, for Jesus, for all of us, is infinite. She has a greater understanding than any other child of the Father. We consider her our Great Sister, but she is much more: the Mother of the Omniverse."

This message goes beyond the limits of most Marian material and opens the suggestion that the ancient Mother Goddess may in some way be involved. While it is obviously not possible to verify unwitnessed apparitions that leave no unexplainable trace, it is nevertheless true that this material is deeply embedded in human mythological tradition.

There are in the gospels numerous references to similar luminous beings. After Christ's resurrection the women who went to the tomb encountered "two men [who] stood by them in shining garments" (Lk. 24:4). The Acts of the Apostles describe the Ascension of Christ into the Heavens as follows: ". . . two men stood by them in white apparel . . ." (Acts 1:10) Jesus himself announced his return "in the clouds," as we read in the Gospel According to St. Matthew, 24:30: "And they shall see the son of man coming in the clouds of heaven . . ."

The Prophet Isaiah asked: "Who are these that fly as a cloud, and as the doves to their windows?" (Is. 60:8) In Fatima the Mother of God appeared "on a small white cloud." Luminous clouds are described in a number of Marian apparitions. The Guadalupe apparition, according to Juan Diego, "seemed to come out of a luminous white cloud hovering over the peak of the Tepeyac."

In Germany one of the most remarkable series of apparitions took place between 1949 and 1952 in Heroldsbach, in Franconia. It was witnessed by eight girls between ten and eleven in age. Tens of thousands of both believers and skeptics came to the scene and many of them observed unusual aerial phenomena. Over twenty thousand people saw a "dance of the sun" on December 18, 1949, after which several other mysterious phenomena were observed. One witness reported, "After the solar event we saw nine large reddish and yellow spheres high above the forest. They remained at the same altitude, moving only slightly. I observed them for about ten minutes, then they suddenly disappeared." Other witnesses described a "bright star" that hovered over the forest and later moved slowly westward. One of them was professor of theology Dr. J. B. Walz, who had come as a critical and rather skeptical observer. He remembered, "Suddenly I heard the crowd shouting, 'Over there, over the forest, a star!' I looked and saw it clearly. 'The star moves! The star moves!' they all said with happy excitement. I observed a bright, nonflickering light that was slowly moving in a horizontal direction to the right. . . . First I believed it was the evening star, but I changed my mind when I saw that it was moving in a straight course."

Something similar happened in Montichiari, Italy, during a series of apparitions. Pilgrims claimed they saw "twelve stars forming a circle" on April 20, 1969: "Then, at some distance, a small, pale disk appeared, growing when approaching us in a horizontal direction. It changed its color and swayed like a lantern in a strong wind. Then it came close to the clouds and seemed to fall down on Earth. Eventually it split into two halves and a cross of light became visible."

What might this mean? Is ours indeed a fallen world, and do the apparitions represent sacred beings attempting to break through to the lost heart of man? Or does the deepest meaning of the experience have to do with the human mind? If so, then there are things about the mind that we *really* don't understand. For example, it can manifest in ways that thousands of people can see at the same time, as happened at Fatima. And as long ago as the sixteenth century it could have extraordinary insight into the workings of human society, as is shown by the vast cultural changes that took place in Mexico as a result of the apparition at Guadalupe.

Unless all the witnesses are simply ignored, it is

necessary to say that at least some of the Marian apparitions are very genuine mysteries. Judging strictly from the number of witnesses involved, it must also be concluded that Fatima is the greatest of these mysteries.

The Secret of Fatima, seen in this light, becomes intensely interesting. Indeed, it has such overwhelming potency that no pope dared to reveal it for eighty years, not even long after the date when it was opened and the time at which it was intended to be read.

Why did the papacy keep this secret? We now know what it is. *The Fatima Secret* is a journey into the inner world of the apparitions and the hidden recesses of the Vatican, to discover the truth.

PREFACE
by MICHAEL HESEMANN

IN ANCIENT TIMES people believed that their destiny was in the hands of the gods. Even kings consulted oracles to learn about their future, and the divine plan for their life.

Judaism was the first prophetic religion. Abraham received a call from God to leave his home and head for the Promised Land. So did Moses, when he liberated his people from slavery in Egypt. Christianity followed this tradition. Paul, its most powerful missionary, was called by an apparition on the way to Damascus.

Today, in an era of enlightened rationalism, we think we have no need for prophets anymore. But are we really masters of our lives, or is there still someone else, a higher intelligence, guiding us? There are many instances in recorded history when "someone" seems to have interfered in human affairs. We prefer to ignore these reports, because they don't seem to fit our concept of reality.

But was it only a hallucination that caused Paul to end his persecution of the Christians and so deeply convinced him that, eventually, he was willing to die for his vision? Was it a legend that caused Constantine the Great to become Rome's first Christian emperor, against the resistance of the powerful Roman senate?

Like the vision of Constantine, who saw an image of the cross in the skies of Italy when he marched against Rome, signs and wonders, miracles and apparitions, have always been part of history. Were they all just superstitious hallucinations, as the skeptics want us to believe? Or are they evidence of divine intervention?

This book tries to prove what we too often have chosen to ignore: that someone, a higher intelligence, controls our evolution, and intervenes in human history through supernatural signs and apparitions.

One of the most important examples of this comes not from the legendary past, but from the twentieth century, and concerns the rise and fall of the Communist empire. The war against Communism was not won on the major stages of world politics, but in a remote village in the mountains of Portugal. It involved neither statesmen nor clergy, but three uneducated, naive peasant children and a luminous white Lady who spoke to them. These were the apparitions at Fatima.

They happened in a year that was more crucial than any other in this war-ridden, sorrowful century. Due to

Communism the world was divided in two halves for more than five decades by an iron curtain, and thrown into a cold war, one of the longest and definitely the most costly in history.

Nineteen seventeen was a year of gathering strength for the three men who would most affect modern history: Lenin, Stalin, and Hitler. It was also the year a supernatural intervention took place that eventually caused the fall of Communism, which was the end result of these men's evil plans for the world. Communism was not defeated by a war, or by the most powerful nuclear arsenal on earth, but by faith alone.

John Paul II was the pope who finally fulfilled the request of Our Lady of Fatima. This man intends to lead mankind in the New Millennium with a very special message, a message of reconciliation and reorientation, the message of Fatima. In November of 1999 he traveled to Portugal to celebrate the beatification of two of the three seer children, in front of a million people and TV cameras from all over the world. It was a symbolic gesture connected with the hope that peace will finally reign on earth, as was predicted by the "white Lady," who, as the thousands who have seen her believe, is the Mother of God.

This is not a religious book. I do not aim to prove the truth of any religious doctrine. I only want to show that there is definite proof that a higher intelligence of some kind staged Fatima and all the other miracles and apparitions that have made history, and intervened in human affairs.

Who is doing this? I have to admit that I first entertained the thought that it could be an extraterrestrial intelligence. On the other hand, it is dangerous to explain one unexplained phenomenon with another one. We have to view the events in Fatima, and the whole era of Marian apparitions, in their own light. Their message is a purely spiritual one, and therefore we can conclude that there is a spiritual intelligence behind them.

However, there is an obvious correlation with the UFO phenomenon. This does not mean that extraterrestrials stage these events as tools to manipulate or even to save us. It could mean that these alien beings, whoever they are, live in a kind of harmony with God and the universe that enables them to fulfill His plans. When Pope John Paul II visited Mexico City on January 22–26, 1999, thousands of witnesses saw and filmed large formations of luminous craft, as if they had come to greet the ailing pontiff. Why wouldn't they do the same thing when the Mother of God appears?

The Madonna appears in many shapes and forms. At times she can appear to be so real, she seems touchable. Other times she is seen as a sphere of light, a manifestation of pure energy. What do these Marian apparitions tell us? Often they include precise and completely fulfilled predictions, both about the future of mankind and the personal fate of the visionaries.

Fatima is more than a tiny village in the Portuguese mountains that became one of the most important places of pilgrimage in the Christian world. Fatima stands for a message that deeply influenced the twentieth century. There are only very few events in the last millennium that had as deep an impact as the message of Fatima. It influenced the secret policy of the Vatican, the smallest but most influential state on earth, from Pope Pius XII to John Paul II, who believes it to be his mission to fulfill the Fatima prophecy. It is part of an overall phenomenon of Marian revelations, which started in the middle of the nineteenth century and are still growing. Never before have there been as many Marian miracles as in the last hundred years, at the threshold of the third millennium.

Michael Hesemann
Düsseldorf, Germany
December 12, 1999

CHAPTER ONE

JOURNEY TO FATIMA

MY LUFTHANSA FLIGHT landed softly at Lisbon Airport. A warm breeze welcomed me as I walked down the gangway and into the bus, which brought me to the terminal. I went through passport control, picked up my luggage, and walked to the taxi stand.

My driver was a young Portuguese with short black hair and skin tanned by the sun. When I told him my destination was Fatima, he said, "You're a pilgrim, aren't you?"

I thought about my reply. What was I really looking for here? "Actually, I'm not. I'm a journalist."

Fatima—what could it offer me? Kitsch and commerce, trading on the faith of millions, as in every place of pilgrimage. Crowds of pilgrims seeking help, praying on their knees that the Holy Virgin might relieve them just a little from the burdens of their lives. Demonstrations of splendor, pomp, and power by the Church. And also, perhaps, an understanding of what really happened eighty years ago in the Portuguese mountain village, eighty miles north of Lisbon, that still keeps so many thousands of pilgrims coming to this place.

Did something supernatural, even divine, actually happen in Fatima? Were the young children who reported seeing the visions of the Virgin mother of Jesus merely naive religious hysterics? Or were the messages they received authentic revelations from a higher place, warnings for the world that had just entered the twentieth century, soon to be shaken and torn by war? I wanted to have the Fatima experience myself, so that I could find the answers to my questions.

For about an hour I rode through the picturesque landscape of Portugal on the highway heading north, passing villages with all the little houses painted white, as well as ruined castles, and the splendid façades of monasteries. There were fresh green pastures, pine forests, olive groves, and oaks. It was a place that seemed to have remained in the more innocent past. The landscape got barer and more mountainous as we approached Fatima. Finally, there it was in front of us: a small village with the elegant basilica towering high above it.

Riding through the streets of Fatima, I was left in no doubt about where the village got its income. Pilgrim buses roared past us. Accommodations for pilgrims were on every corner, from simple hostels to four-star hotels. Dozens of shops offered statues of the Virgin, made out of plastic, ceramic, and wood. There were piles of candles, rosaries, and medals for sale.

After I checked into my hotel, I walked through the *sanctuario,* or sanctuary of Fatima. It was September 12, 1996, the seventy-ninth anniversary of the fifth apparition. I was surrounded by hundreds, if not thousands, of pilgrims. Some had candles in their hands, others said the rosary as they walked along. The low murmur of praying voices filled the air.

The great square in front of the basilica reminded me of St. Peter's Square in Rome. The basilica is set in a park, surrounded by green trees and bushes. I passed the entrance, where signs are posted reminding tourists of the devotions going on inside.

The narrow basilica is built on an elevation, with stairs going down toward the square in all directions, as if welcoming pilgrims from all over the world. To the left is the small chapel that was erected at the Virgin's request. Between this chapel and the basilica, surrounded by a wall, is the huge oak tree over which the "White Lady" once appeared.

Pilgrims surrounded the chapel on their knees. Old country women with weathered faces, black dresses, and head scarves wore homemade knee pads so that they could stay on their knees for a longer time. There were well-dressed people on their knees as well, including elegant ladies from the best families in Italy, gentlemen in navy-blue blazers, and teen-agers in blue jeans or traditional costumes.

All offered their prayers to the statue of Our Lady of Fatima, which stood, protected by a glass box, on a pedestal in front of the chapel. Next to it hundreds of sac-rificial candles burned in a wall of metallic holders, melt-ing into one another, as columns of black smoke ascended into heaven.

I couldn't begin to guess how many prayers are said here every day. When the Virgin appeared to the three shepherd children, Lúcia, Jacinta, and Francisco, nearly eighty years ago, she told them to say the rosary often, and the pilgrims who come here have faithfully kept this tradition.

I began to wonder about how authentic the legends of Fatima are that are printed in the many book-lets and tracts for sale in the tourist shops that fill this village.

I've read all the books and know all the speculations about the mysterious "Third Secret" of Fatima. I've traveled to Rome many times from my home in Ger-many, and spoken with Vatican insiders, about the con-tents of the Third Secret. I've met people who claim that the Virgin appeared personally to them, and others who bear the mysterious, bleeding "stigmata" on their bodies, wounds in their hands and feet in the same places where nails were driven into the body of Jesus at the crucifixion. I'd visited the sights of other apparitions, in Mexico, Italy, Austria, Hungary, Spain, Bosnia, Germany, and the United States.

Based on eyewitness testimonies I've tried to reconstruct the Fatima events as exactly and carefully as possible, and to show how deeply these visions have influenced the history of the twentieth century. Fatima had a deep impact on the secret policies of the Vatican, which is the smallest state, yet the most influential superpower, on earth. All the popes of this century have been aware of the Virgin's messages, from Pope Pius XII up to John Paul II, who has announced that it is his mission to fulfill the prophecy of Fatima.

The Fatima visions cannot be seen as an isolated event. They are part of a larger phenomenon of Marian visions, which began in the mid-nineteenth century and have increased in frequency ever since. The warnings given to us by the Marian apparitions are similar to the warnings received from UFO visitors. Both seem to be telling us that we have reached a crucial moment in human evolution, where we stand at a point between self-destruction and a world of new spiritual possibilities.

John Paul II is expected to announce that Catholic doctrine of the third millennium will be mainly dictated by the revelations of these apparitions. In November 1999 he traveled to Portugal to announce the beatification of two of the three children who saw the Fatima vision, in front of a million people and TV cameras from all over the world. The ceremony took place on May 13, 2000.

It might surprise many Catholics to know that a belief in the existence of extraterrestrial intelligence is in
no way frowned upon by Catholic doctrine. Father
Francis J. Connell, former dean of theology of
the Catholic University of America, stated in the
November 7, 1957, issue of the *Denver Register*
that "theologians have never dared to limit the omni-
potence of God to the creation of the world we know.

"If God did create other rational beings," he continued, "theologians can imagine a variety of states in
which they might exist. These beings could have received from God the same supernatural and preternatural
gifts given to Adam and Eve and could never have lost
them. They might be intellectually and physically superior to us."

A couple of years ago, in a discussion about the
controversial *Alien Autopsy* TV special on Italian National Television, I met Monsignore Corrado Balducci
for the first time. He has been a high-ranking member of
the Vatican for fifty-two years and is also an expert on
demonology, a branch of Catholic theology dealing with
the supernatural. For several years he worked as an exor-
cist in the Vatican for Pope Paul VI. Balducci is well informed about the Fatima events, and published the text
of the alleged "Third Secret" in 1978 in the Sunday edition of the Vatican's official newspaper, *L'Osservatore
Romano.*

During the next few years we developed a close
friendship, and in 1997 Monsignor Balducci gave me an

interview that even made headlines in the London *Times*. In this interview he states that he believes UFOs are real, that contacts happen, and that this belief does not contradict Catholic doctrine. On the other hand, he does not go along with the idea that extraterrestrials could be the angels of the Bible.

Skeptics tend to refute the reality of the Fatima apparitions as projections of the unconscious, hallucinations, or religious hysteria. Although it may be possible to explain some of the miraculous healings as psychosomatic in nature, there are three predictions that cannot be explained away. First, there is the impressive "miracle of the sun," which was observed by more than fifty thousand eyewitnesses. The sun suddenly began to turn a series of bright colors, then rotated rapidly and seemed about to crash into the earth. This was seen even in the neighboring villages, which excludes the possibility of mass hysteria.

Second, there were the predictions about political and meteorological events that were far beyond the imaginations of three young uneducated children: the Russian Revolution, the spread of Communism, and World War II. Third, the promise of the Madonna that the spread of Communism could be stopped came true. The beginning of the end of the Soviet Union started within a year after the election of the first pope from a Communist country, John Paul II.

Many of the Fatima messages I quote may

seem childish or old-fashioned, but that doesn't mean they should be ignored. After all, they were given to children, and perhaps we are all childlike when it comes to the great mysteries of life and religion.

The secular confusion of our times was predicted by the "White Lady" who appeared at Fatima. In the modern age, when many people have turned their backs on religion, we tend to forget that there is indeed a world of the unknown, even the divine—that the universe is spiritual, and not just physical.

This "other" world breaks through the barriers into our everyday lives in ways as diverse as UFO phenomena and Marian apparitions. These events can be documented and researched, using scientific methods. We don't need to dismiss them simply because they don't have a place in our modern worldview.

We must be careful not to become like the church representatives of the seventeenth century, who were not willing to look through the telescope of Galileo Galilei, for fear that their notions of what was real would be proven false.

Whoever it is who is out there, they are trying to communicate with us. We are not alone.

CHAPTER TWO

A VISION
IN PORTUGAL

IT WAS AUGUST 17, 1959, in Castelgondolfo, Italy, the summer residence of the pope. "There you are!" exclaimed the man in the white soutane, when he saw the messenger from Rome. "Do you have it with you?"

"Yes, Your Holiness," answered the monk, who was dressed entirely in black, except for his white clerical collar. He handed him an envelope.

A smile spread over the face of Pope John XXIII. "I think I'll wait a bit before opening it. I want to read it when my confessor is here." Father Paul Philippe bowed respectfully. He had done his job of bringing to Castelgondolfo what was perhaps the most explosive document in the Christian world. The pope would decide whether the document could be published next year.

Pope John waited four days, until Friday, August 21,

before breaking the seal on the envelope, which bore the insignia of the bishop of Leiria. He had arranged for a Vatican interpreter to be present, in case there was difficulty understanding the Portuguese text. Sitting in a closed room, with only the interpreter and his confessor, Monsignor Alfredo Cavagna, present, the pope read the words that Sister Lúcia had written down fifteen years before.

When Lúcia dos Santos was a child, she was no different from many others who lived in that wild and mountainous district of Portugal known as the Serra de Aire. She was a typical farmer's daughter, fond of singing, dancing, and playing with her friends. She loved to dress up in her mother's colorful shawls and put on the costume jewelry she found in the dresser drawer. She was high spirited and talkative, and liked to be the center of attention.

She wasn't a pretty child. She was stocky, with a flat nose, wide mouth, and thick black eyebrows above deep black eyes. Her face was framed by a mane of heavy black hair, parted in the middle.

Lúcia was born on March 22, 1907, the last of seven children of António and Maria Rosa dos Santos of Aljustrel, a hamlet of only eighteen houses, which formed a tiny green oasis in the middle of the barren Serra de Aire.

Her parents were simple farmers, honest and deeply religious. They taught their daughter to pray the rosary and to say grace at meals. During one of his sermons the local priest said that dancing was sinful, and from that day on Lúcia was not permitted to take part in any of the local dances.

Her cousin Francisco was born on June 11, 1908. The sixth child of Manuel Pedro Marto and his wife Olimpia, he was a sturdy boy with a round, plump face that always had a smile on it. He was quiet, good natured, and patient, and in the presence of his adored cousin Lúcia, he seemed to have no will of his own. The people in the village used to say that he was a dreamer, like his father. He liked to stay up late, gazing at the stars.

Francisco's sister Jacinta was born exactly twenty-one months after him, on March 11, 1910. The people in the village called her "the little angel." She had a small round face with fine features. She loved flowers, which she would often pick to make garlands for herself and her cousin. She loved nature and often joined her brother in his star gazing. When the sheep gave birth to lambs, she would spend hours petting the newborns, and gave them special names.

When Jacinta was older, her parents sent her and her brother to Lúcia, who was expected to look after them. Later on, all three children were given the job of driving their herds of sheep to the meadows for grazing.

Many people have asked why these three simple children were chosen to witness a miracle. There seems to be nothing special about them at all. They were no more religious than the other children of local farmers. They said the rosary daily as they were told to do, but they rattled off the words quickly, letting the beads rush past their fingers, so they could go back outside to play.

The days began early for Francisco and Jacinta, even before the sun had risen. After their mother woke them up, they would quickly wash their faces and hands, and eat their breakfast, which was usually vegetable or rice soup, with some olive oil and homemade bread. Their mother would then give them their lunches, containing bread, olives, and sardines or dried fish, and their working day began. They would drive the sheep out of the pen and take them to the grazing pastures.

On the way they would meet up with Lúcia, who would join them with her family's herd. The children would watch the sheep and play together until sundown, then they would collect their sheep and drive them home, where the evening meal would be waiting for them. After a last quickly murmured prayer they would lie down on their straw mattresses, tired but happy.

In their small world they were not aware of what was going on around them in the rest of Europe, where one of the longest and bloodiest wars in history was raging. They didn't know that their own country, Portugal, was in a state of chaos.

At the beginning of the twentieth century the Portuguese monarchy was weak. In 1907 the prime minister was determined to bring about the downfall of the monarchy. On February 1, 1908, King Charles I was gunned down in the marketplace in Lisbon by terrorists from a radical group. Eighteen-year-old Emanuel, who became the successor to the throne, tried to reach an understanding with the republicans. But during the night of October 3, 1910, twenty members of an armed group stormed the barracks of the 16th Infantry Regiment in a surprise attack and the entire arsenal fell into the hands of the revolutionists. A republic was proclaimed in the city hall of Lisbon. A provisional government was established, and the royal family fled to Gibraltar.

The first aim of the republicans was to destroy the authority of the clergy, because they had been allied with the monarchy. Laws were passed to forbid the establishment of religious orders and expel the Jesuits. The religious oath taken at courts of justice was abolished, and professors no longer had to defend the dogma of the church. All religious holidays were canceled. On Christmas Day marriage was declared to be a purely civil contract and on the last day of the year priests were forbidden, under threat of imprisonment, to give religious instruction or wear clerical clothes in public.

The minister of justice, Alfonso Costa, went so far as to say, "The Catholic religion, the main cause of the miserable lives of the people, will be eradicated in Portugal within two generations."

But what happened in Portugal was only the start of a decade that would push the whole of Europe into war and bring about the downfall of three of its largest monarchies.

On June 28, 1914, the crown prince of the Austro-Hungarian empire, Archduke Franz Ferdinand, was shot to death in Sarajevo by a nineteen-year-old student. At that time nobody thought that this bloody deed, interpreted as an act of revenge for the oppression of the Serbs, would change the face of the old world so completely.

Austria declared war on Serbia, causing her ally, Russia, to mobilize her armies. Germany reacted by marching against France, causing Britain to declare war on the German Reich. The allied troops of France and England succeeded in stopping the German advance after four weeks, but not until over six hundred thousand German and French soldiers lost their lives.

Eventually Britain succeeded in getting the United States to join the conflict. The U.S. officially declared war on Germany on April 6, 1917.

Meanwhile, Russia was in turmoil. The people joined with the army in revolt against the czar and imprisoned him, along with his family. The charismatic leader Vladimir Lenin returned from exile and gathered support for his final step to power.

By the time the First World War ended a year later, eight million people were dead.

During this period Portugal was in a state of political turmoil. Between 1911 and 1926 there were eight presidents, forty-four governments, and twenty revolutions.

But the simple people in the Serra de Aire knew little about these struggles. They did know that a terrible war was being waged in Europe, and they feared for the lives of their sons who had been drafted into the army. The children sensed the anxiety of their parents, but the threat of war was too distant to affect their daily lives.

On a hot summer day in 1915 Lúcia and three other girls of about the same age were saying their prayers while their sheep peacefully grazed. Lúcia raised her eyes and looked over the valley. There was a white cloud above it, and to her surprise it took on the shape of a human being, then disappeared.

"Did you see that?" she asked her companions. They had seen it too. None of them could explain what had happened. When the children told their parents about it that evening, no one took them seriously. Perhaps it was some kind of smoke, or the girls had just imagined it. But this phenomenon repeated itself twice during the following days and on both occasions it was when they were saying their midday prayers. The children wondered why the smoke always took on the shape of a person, but they did not speak about this to anyone else, since their parents had already told them it was nothing.

Lúcia might have forgotten this incident, if it had not been the beginning of a series of visions that were to change her life completely and eventually make history. Several months later, in the spring of 1916, Lúcia, Francisco, and Jacinta were watching their herds on the eastern slope of the Loca do Cabeso mountain. It was a cool, wet morning and it was drizzling. They climbed up the slope looking for shelter from the rain. Finally they arrived at a cave, which was in the middle of an olive grove, and had a nice view over the village of Aljustrel.

They remained there even after the sun came out again. As usual, they said their prayers at noon, then ate their lunch. Lúcia described what happened after that.

"We had been playing for some time when suddenly, although it was a calm day, a strong wind started shaking the trees. We looked upward and saw this figure of a boy, about fourteen or fifteen years old, whiter than snow. The sun made him look transparent, as if he were made of crystal. He was beautiful. The closer he came, the better we could see his features. We were surprised and totally enchanted. We didn't say a word.

"He said, 'Don't be afraid! I am the angel of peace. Pray with me.' He knelt on the ground and bent down till his forehead touched the earth. We did the same thing and prayed with him. Then he disappeared."

Something strange and supernatural seemed to remain in the air long after the figure disappeared. The children stood still, filled with astonishment, as if they had been taken to another world in which time did not exist. Gradually they came back to themselves, but their heads were still filled with the image of the angel.

When they returned to the same spot the next day, the magic was still in the air, as if the apparition had opened a door to another dimension. The children were convinced they should keep their experience secret, because it was too precious to be spoiled by the gossip and teasing of their playmates. But even the most wonderful memories fade with time, and the children soon returned to their everyday lives as if nothing had happened.

Summer came, and the days grew hotter and drier. The children woke up earlier so they could take the sheep out in time for them to feed on grass that was still wet with dew. At midday they had to seek shelter from the heat in the shade of fig trees or olive or almond trees.

One day the children decided to go back to the cave in the olive grove, because it gave them shelter from the sun, and also revived memories of their vision. It was about time for their siesta when the angel appeared again. Lúcia recalled, "Suddenly the same angel was in front of us. He said, 'What are you doing? Pray! Pray, pray! Pray without stopping, pray and offer sacrifices.' "

"How do we offer sacrifices?" Lúcia asked.

"Make sacrifices from your ordinary lives." Lúcia and Jacinta heard these words, but not Francisco, who only saw the angel. All three were so stunned that they could not speak about the incident at all. It wasn't until the next day that Francisco got up enough courage to ask Lúcia what the angel had said. She found herself unable to tell him and sent him to Jacinta, but she couldn't speak about it either. The day after that Lúcia managed to tell Francisco what she had heard. But he did not understand the message.

The children found that it wasn't easy to follow the angel's instructions. They tried to fulfill them by avoiding some of the things they liked to do. They repeated their prayers for hours, with their foreheads touching the ground.

Late in August the angel showed himself for the third

time. This time the children were on the mountain slope between Preguiera and Lapa de Cabeco, overlooking Aljustrel. It was noon and they were saying their prayers the way the angel had told them to. Lúcia writes, "While we were praying, the angel appeared for the third time. He held a chalice in his hand, and above it was a consecrated host, with drops of blood falling from it into the chalice. He let go of the chalice and the host, and they floated in the air by themselves, then he knelt down and prayed.

"Then he stood up and took hold of the chalice and the host once more. He gave me the host and gave Jacinta and Francisco the contents of the chalice to drink. Then he knelt down again and prayed before he disappeared."

Once more it took a little time before the children returned to normal. They were exhausted, but at the same time they were filled with a deep sense of happiness. It was as if they had returned from a state of spiritual ecstasy. The angel's appearance led the three little shepherds into a magical new world of visions and revelations.

There has been much discussion about what could have been behind the visions of Fatima. Was it hysteria, or even mental illness? But the way the children's descriptions agreed with one another, their deep inner feelings afterward, and the powerful symbols that were involved, all make this seem unlikely. How could innocent, uneducated children make up these kinds of things?

Was it wishful thinking, motivated by their religious training? These were down-to-earth farm children, who liked playing better than praying. They had wanted to forget the first of these appearances.

Were the visions, as some writers have suggested, holographic images projected by an alien intelligence? People who have UFO experiences often find themselves spiritually transformed afterward. Some abductees even develop healing abilities.

When the first series of apparitions was over, the children returned to their everyday lives. The vision of the angel and his instructions gradually faded in their memories, as their lives returned to their daily chores and the joys of childhood.

Soon winter came and, along with it, the festivities of Christmas. Next, the cold storms of winter gave way to the gentle rain of April. Plants burst out of the earth, the meadows were covered with green grass, and the bare branches of the trees were soon covered with leaves and blossoms. The stony slopes of the Serra were once more filled with life and again it was time to take the sheep out to their pastures, where they would give birth to lambs. The children loved to see the lambs curiously but timidly explore the meadows on their shaky legs.

Lúcia, Francisco, and Jacinta did not know that 1917 would become a special year for them and for religious people everywhere. It was a time of terror in the world. Far away in Russia, Vladimir Ilyich Lenin was at that moment planning the atheistic Soviet regime of the future. Meanwhile, in the highlands of Portugal, the power of religion was revealing itself to mankind.

CHAPTER THREE

A WOMAN CLOTHED
WITH THE SUN

ON SUNDAY, MAY 13, 1917, the three children attended mass at the local church, as they always did. Afterward they went out with the sheep. They were in no hurry and wandered slowly over the stony paths, allowing their sheep to graze along the roadside, so by the time they reached their destination, the sun was high up in the sky. When the bells in the village rang at noon, they hurried to unpack their lunches, which on Sundays always had something special in them. After they finished eating, they drove the sheep to a fresh grazing area, and started playing some of their favorite games.

The hamlet of Aljustrel, where Lúcia, Jacinta, and Francisco lived, was part of the village of Fatima, which got its name from a legend. When the Moors ruled the south of the Iberian Peninsula, Christian warriors repeatedly attacked the Moslems using guerrilla tactics. One of these fighters was Gonçalo Hermingues, who led an army of Christian soldiers.

On June 24, 1158, a group of Moslem knights and their ladies rode out from the provincial capital Al-Kasar (today called Alcácer do Sal) to the banks of the River Sado for a picnic. They were suddenly raided by Gonçalo Hermingues and his army. During the surprise attack most of the Arab knights were killed, and the survivors and all the women were taken prisoner. One of them was the daughter of the Muslim prince of Al-Kasar, who was named Fatima, after the favorite daughter of the prophet Mohammed.

Gonçalo fell in love with the beautiful princess, and she, impressed by his bravery, was eventually willing to convert to Christianity and marry him.

Unfortunately, the lovely Fatima died young. Her heartbroken husband sought solace in a monastery near Qureana. The abbot of the monastery permitted him to bury his wife in a little church nearby. From that day on the village in which the church stood was called Fatima, after the princess. At the beginning of the twentieth century this village in the mountains, together with all the hamlets surrounding it, had a total population of only about two thousand people.

It is interesting to note that a Christian place with the name of the daughter of Mohammed should become so important to the faith of the world. "Nothing comes from heaven that has no meaning," the theologian Monsignor Fulton Sheen said, referring to this.

"In the face of rationalism Fatima is one of the altars of the world on which the Mother of God calls to both Christian and Islamic communities," said the Frenchman Charles Barzel.

In fact, Islam reveres Mary, just as Christianity does. The Twenty-first Sutra of the Koran, verses ninety-one and ninety-two, says, "Remember her who had preserved her virginity but whom we had touched with our spirit and created her son to be a sign of wonder for the whole world."

Two miles away from Fatima is a piece of land called Cova da Íria, which belonged to Lúcia's parents. It means "Irene's Cove," named after the Portuguese saint Irene. It's a grassy depression about fifteen hundred feet in diameter, surrounded by mountains, which forms a natural amphitheater. It was to this sheltered meadow that Lúcia, Jacinta, and Francisco drove their sheep to graze on that memorable day.

Suddenly, they were interrupted by a dazzling flash of light. They assumed it was lightning and were worried that a storm was coming, for then they would have to head for home right away.

Although no clouds could be seen in the blue sky above them, Lúcia didn't like the look of things, and decided they should start back home, in case the weather was about to change. The other two were ready to follow her, but they had barely turned around when a second beam of light flashed in the sky. They all turned toward the place where the light was coming from, and what they saw made them gasp with astonishment.

"There was an oak tree and a Lady dressed completely in white, brighter than the sun, was floating above its top," Lúcia said later. "She had rays of light around her, like you see when the sun shines through a glass filled with water, but much, much brighter. We stood still, shocked by what we saw. We were so close that we were inside the circle of light that radiated out from her. She was less than five feet away."

The Lady seemed to be around eighteen years old. She was about four feet tall and had dark eyes. Her long dress was pure white, tied at the neck with a golden ribbon. It reached down to her feet, which barely skimmed the tops of the trees. A white hooded cloak, bordered in gold, covered her head and framed her whole body. Her hands were folded in front of her as if in prayer, and they held a rosary of shining white beads with a silver cross dangling from the bottom. She wore a long necklace, which reached to her waist, and had a round pendant hanging from it. Bright light surrounded her head, but her lovely face seemed filled with sorrow.

"Don't be afraid," she said, "I won't hurt you." She spoke in a soft voice, which took away all Lúcia's fear.

"Where are you from?" she asked her.

"I am from heaven," answered the mysterious Lady.

"And what are you doing in this world?" asked the child, simply.

"I am here to ask you to come to this place on the thirteenth day of every month, during the next six months, at the same time as today. Then I'll tell you who I am and what I want. After that I'll come here once more, for the seventh time."

"Will I also go to heaven?"

"Certainly."

"And Jacinta?"

"Yes, she will too."

"And Francisco?"

"Yes, he will also. But he must pray a lot of rosaries before that."

With the same childish simplicity Lúcia asked about two of her friends who had died. "Are they already in heaven?"

"Yes."

"Can you tell me if the war will go on for a long time or will it come to an end soon?"

"I cannot tell you that now, just as I cannot tell you what I want."

Lúcia swallowed rather unhappily. Then the radiant Lady asked her, "Are you prepared to offer yourself to God, and to accept all the sufferings He will send you to help make up for the sins of the world?"

"Yes, we are ready!" answered Lúcia, speaking for the other two children as well.

"You will have to suffer a great deal," the Lady said, "but the grace of God will give you the strength to bear it." With these words she opened her hands for the first time, and an even brighter light shot out from them and went straight toward the three children.

"We saw that we were the children of this light, more clearly than if we had looked into the best mirrors in the world," wrote Lúcia later. Instinctively, all three children knelt down and began to pray.

"Pray the rosary daily to end the war and bring peace to the world," the figure told them. Then she rose up slowly and moved toward the east, finally disappearing when she was far away. "The light all around her seemed to open a path for her through the sky," said Lúcia.

When the vision began to fade away, they heard a dull explosive noise that sounded "like a rocket exploding in the distance" or like a kind of underground thunder coming from the oak. Lúcia jumped up and stretched out her arms toward the east, crying out, "Look, she's leaving!"

Afterward, the children stood, petrified, staring in the direction where the Lady had disappeared. It took some time for them to gradually become aware once more of the real world that surrounded them. Everything was quiet, the sun was shining, and there was no wind. Suddenly the same thought rushed through the heads of all three children at once: "The sheep!" Lúcia ran quickly to the nearby field where they had strayed, and was relieved to find the owner had driven them out of his field before they could do any damage there.

The children kept silent for a while, then slowly began to talk about what they had seen and heard. "What a beautiful, beautiful Lady she was," repeated Jacinta, over and over again.

It turned out that only Lúcia had spoken to the Lady. Jacinta had only listened, and Francisco had only seen her lips move. He couldn't hear anything that she or Lúcia said. It had all taken about ten minutes.

But Lúcia felt sad, because hadn't the Lady said that they would have to go through a lot of suffering?

The children decided not to tell anyone about this vision. Lúcia remembered the ridicule she'd had to face when she told her family about the vision of the angel.

"Oh, how beautiful she was!" Jacinta kept saying. Lúcia was afraid Jacinta would not be able to keep her mouth shut for very long. But Jacinta reassured her, saying, "No, no, I won't tell anyone."

Francisco said very little. He was hurt that the Lady had not talked to him at all, and that he couldn't hear her speaking. And he thought she'd given him a slightly reproving look as well.

The sun had sunk low in the sky before the children finally decided to go home. They quickly drove their sheep together and set off on the way to Aljustrel. Before Lúcia parted from them, she reminded her friends once more to keep absolutely quiet about the incident.

"We won't tell anyone!" they promised.

But Jacinta had barely gotten home before she forgot her promise. She always told her mother everything and never kept secrets. She tried to keep silent but finally couldn't control herself anymore. She ran to her mother, grabbed her around her knees, and cried out excitedly, "Mama, I saw Our Dear Lady in the Cova today!"

Senhora Marto laughed at her daughter. "Oh, yes, you certainly did," she said, "and you are a saint now, for you can see the Mother of God!"

Jacinta was crushed by these words. Her mother didn't believe her. She began to regret not having kept her promise.

"But I really saw her, Mother," she said softly, and added a while later, "Mama, I'll pray the rosary with Francisco daily. The Mother of God told us to. We have to say the rosary every day, that's what she wants."

Later on, during the evening meal, Senhora Marto asked her daughter to tell about how and where she had seen the Madonna. The story came bubbling out of the girl. She told her whole family about the lightning, about the glorious light that was so bright it almost hurt their eyes, the beautiful Lady dressed all in white, and the golden necklace that reached down to her waist with a radiant ball hanging at the end of it. When she said the Lady had her hands folded, Jacinta jumped up and folded her hands in front of her, imitating the pose.

Francisco confirmed her story. Their brothers and sisters started teasing them, but finally their father, Ti Marto, who was the thoughtful one in the family, raised his voice and said, "Since the beginning of the world the Mother of God has appeared at different times and places. If this never happened, the world would be in a worse state than it is today. God is great. We don't understand everything He does, but may His will be done."

These words made a deep impression on the family and they finished their soup in silence.

The next morning Senhora Marto began to gossip about the vision to everyone in the village. Soon the rumors reached Lúcia's mother, who questioned her daughter. Reluctantly, Lúcia affirmed that she, too, had seen the Mother of God. She was sad that Jacinta had not been able to keep her mouth shut. Maria Rosa could not believe her, and decided her youngest daughter had suddenly become a liar.

The children were filled with anxiety whenever they spoke about the incident during the following days. Their playful and carefree childhood seemed to be over. Lúcia began to feel like a martyr. As far as her father was concerned, the whole thing was nonsense. Her mother tried in every possible way to make Lúcia take it all back and confess that she had made up the story.

She kept on making accusations until the little girl, in tears, begged her on her knees to stop. When Maria Rosa found that punishment couldn't make her daughter retract her story, she dragged Lúcia to the village priest, Father Ferreira. On the way she threatened her, saying, "When you get there, beg for forgiveness and confess to him that you've been telling lies. Otherwise I will shut you up in a black hole for the rest of your life!"

But the efforts of the priest were also in vain. Lúcia stuck to her story about what she had seen.

The story spread through the whole region long before June 13 arrived, the day the Lady was to meet with them again. Over fifty people had gathered near the oak tree, starting early that morning. Following the instructions of the "White Lady," Lúcia, Jacinta, and Francisco arrived about eleven o'clock. Their parents had refused to come with them, because they were afraid of being embarrassed if the whole thing turned out to be a fraud.

June 13 was the feast of Saint Anthony and was usually celebrated in Fatima with bell ringing, a colorful procession, and free meals for five hundred people. The farmers' families would come in their ox-drawn carts decorated with flowers and colorful banners. Food and money would be distributed to the poor. The carriages were driven to the church, where the priest would bless them. Lúcia loved this feast, and secretly her mother had hoped that the excitement would make Lúcia forget the whole affair at the Cova da Íria. But along with Jacinta and Francisco, Lúcia had decided to give up celebrating the Feast of Saint Anthony as a sacrifice for the sake of the Mother of God.

"When it was time, the children came to the Cova," said a woman witness later, describing the events of that day. "They knelt down under the big oak tree and recited the prayers of the rosary. When they finished, Lúcia stood up, straightened the scarf on her head, and smoothed her shawl, as if she were going to church, and turned toward the east, where she expected to see the vision.

"The people standing around asked whether they would have to wait long, but the girl said no. The other two children said there was still time to pray the rosary once more, but Lúcia replied, 'The lightning has flashed already, the Lady is coming.' She ran quickly to the little oak tree, followed by the other two."

Another witness was Senhora Maria dos Santos Carreira of Fatima, who lived about ten minutes away. She and her seventeen-year-old handicapped son were the first persons to reach the Cova that morning.

"Soon more and more people came," she said, "and at about eleven o'clock the children the Lady had appeared to arrived. They came with other children and also people from quite far away like Torres Novas or Outeiro. We all went to the little oak tree. Lúcia stood about ten feet away from the tree and looked toward the east. It was very quiet. I asked her, 'Where is the tree where the Lady appeared?'

" 'It's this one here,' she said, and went over and laid her hand on it. It was a pretty little tree about three feet tall with evenly growing branches. Lúcia moved away from the tree, looked in the direction of Fatima, and then sat down in the shade of a fig tree nearby. The children joined her."

Lúcia described what happened after that this way: "After Jacinta, Francisco, and I recited the rosary, together with some other people, we saw the light that we call lightning again. Then the Lady was above the oak tree, the same way it all happened in May.

" 'What do you want from me?' I asked.

" 'I want all three of you to recite the prayers of the rosary every day and I want you to learn to read and write. After that I'll tell you what I really want.'

"When I asked her to heal a certain sick person, she answered, 'If he opens his heart to Jesus Christ, he will be cured within the year.'

" 'Please, take us with you to heaven.'

" 'Yes, I shall take Jacinta and Francisco with me to heaven soon, but you have to stay here for a while longer. Jesus wants to make use of you to help people understand and love me.' "

Lúcia could barely pay attention to this, for she was shocked to learn that Jacinta and Francisco would soon die.

"Will I be left here alone?" she asked sadly.

"No, my child. Are you suffering very much? Don't let yourself be discouraged. I shall never leave you."

Lúcia recalled, "When she spoke these last words, she opened her hands and for the second time we saw the wonderful light come out of them. I saw Jacinta and Francisco in a beam of light, going up to heaven, and myself in a beam of light that was pouring down on earth."

Many witnesses later described how they had not only heard Lúcia's voice, but also heard a mysterious murmur in reply. Maria dos Santos Carreira described it, "as if I heard a voice from a great distance, something like the humming of a bee," but she could not make out the words themselves. When the vision began to fade away, they heard a dull explosion, which some described as being "like a rocket exploding in the distance" and others as a kind of underground thunder that came out of the oak tree. At this moment Lúcia jumped up and, stretching out her arms toward the east, called out, "Look, she's leaving!"

Maria Carreira said, "We saw only a little cloud above the tree, that rose up slowly and moved off toward the east. Some of us lost sight of it, but others said they could still see it, until finally it disappeared completely. The children stood silently looking toward the place where it had been, and Lúcia said, 'Now we can't see her anymore. She has gone back to heaven and the door has closed.'

"We looked at the little tree again and, to our surprise, found that the branches on the top of it, which had been growing straight up, were now bent toward the east, as if someone had been standing on them."

One of the other witnesses confirmed this, saying, "The oak tree was covered with young leaves. The tender twigs got bent during the vision as if the weight of the Lady had rested on them. After Lúcia said she had returned to heaven, we noticed that all the leaves and twigs were bent toward the east, as if the hem of her cloak had been drawn across them."

Maria dos Santos said, "We began to break off twigs from the tree, but Lúcia told us to only take the ones from the bottom, which had not been in contact with the Lady.

Someone suggested that we all pray the rosary before going home, so we started off toward Fatima reciting the prayers of the rosary. We arrived just as the festival procession was being formed. People wanted to know where we had been, and we told them we had been at the Cova and how happy we were to have gone there. Many of them were sad that they had missed something so very important, but by then it was too late."

The vision had survived its first test, and news of the mysterious phenomenon spread like wildfire throughout the Serra de Aire.

CHAPTER FOUR

THE THREE SECRETS

ON JULY 13, 1917, the number of witnesses increased from the fifty curious people who had come on the previous occasion, to a throng of almost three thousand pilgrims. Some came from far away. Many had arrived the previous evening on foot or in donkey carts, and spent the night under the open sky, wrapped up in blankets. Someone put up a wooden arch with a cross on it to mark the site of the apparition. Repeating the rosary and exchanging the latest gossip about the three children, the pilgrims waited impatiently for noon, when the Mother of God had promised to appear. They had no idea that Lúcia was almost prevented from coming to the oak this time.

The day after the previous appearance, on June 13, Lúcia's mother again took her daughter to the priest Father Ferreira at the rectory in Fatima, because he wanted to have another personal talk with Lúcia. Jacinta and Francisco went along. The priest listened to the story of the children in disbelief, and was annoyed that there were details that they either would not or could not tell him.

Finally he said, "It could be a trick of the devil. We will wait and see." His words hurt Lúcia, because they went against what she believed in. For the people in the village the priest was a representative of God and had great authority. Lúcia began to doubt that what she had seen was real.

Her two friends tried to reassure her. "That was certainly not the devil!" they said. "The devil is ugly and lives under the earth. The Lady was wonderfully beautiful and went up toward heaven."

But Lúcia hardly paid attention to them. She fell into a state of lethargy and despair. She had nightmares, and she was almost tempted to say she had lied, to put an end to the whole thing. But Jacinta said, "Don't do it! You know that lying is a sin."

Lúcia's mother did everything she could to increase Lúcia's doubts. As July 13 approached, she repeated, "The devil is sure to be there on that day."

On the evening of July 12 Lúcia went to Jacinta and Francisco and said that she wouldn't go with them to the Cova. But the other two told her, "We'll go. The Lady has ordered us to come."

As the day stretched toward noon, Lúcia found it more and more impossible to stay at home. She ran to

Jacinta's house and found the two children kneeling before their beds, praying and weeping.

"Aren't you going?" she asked them. They said, "Without you we don't have the courage to go. Please come with us."

Lúcia answered, "Yes, I'll go with you." And in that moment she felt as if a weight had fallen from her shoulders.

Soon afterward, both Olimpia and Maria Rosa discovered their children were not at home. They knew where to find them, and so together with Ti Marto they went to the Cova da Íria. When they got there, they found the three children surrounded by hundreds of people.

Ti Marto recollected later, "There was a huge crowd, but then two men, one from Ramilla and one from here, built a barrier around the children to protect them. When the men saw me, they took me by the arm and shouted out, 'Here is the father of the children, allow him to get through.' That's how I was able to join my Jacinta.

"A little farther away Lúcia was kneeling on the ground, saying the rosary. The crowd repeated the words after her. When they finished, she jumped up so quickly, it was as if she was being pulled up by invisible hands. She looked to the east and called out, 'Close your umbrellas'—many people had had them open for protection against the sun—'Our Dear Lady is coming!' I strained my eyes but could see nothing. Then I saw what looked like a very small gray cloud above the oak tree. The heat had gone down and a pleasant breeze was blowing, not at all like it usually is in high summer.

"The people were so silent, I could have heard a needle hitting the ground. Then I heard a humming sound, but could not make out any words. I imagine that's how a telephone sounds, although I've never spoken on the telephone in my life. I asked myself what it could be, and was it close, or far away? For me, these were signs that this was a miracle."

When Lúcia saw the glorious figure that once more appeared above the tree, all her doubts vanished. She stood spellbound, fascinated by the beauty of the Lady, and stared without being able to utter a single word. Jacinta became impatient and said, "Lúcia, say something! Can't you see that the Lady is here and wants to talk to you?"

Finally Lúcia asked, "What does Your Grace wish of me?"

"I want you to come here on the thirteenth of next month and to continue to pray the rosary every day, to bring peace to the world and the end of the war."

Lúcia remembered that some of the pilgrims had asked her to beg the Mother of God for help and healing. "I would like to ask you to tell us who you are and to perform a miracle so that everyone will believe that you appear to us," she said.

"Continue to come here every month, as I said. In October I will tell you who I am and what I wish, and I will also perform a miracle, so that everyone who sees it will believe," replied the Lady.

After that she showed the children a vision, which later came to be known as "the First Secret of Fatima."

"With these words," recalled Lúcia later, "the Lady opened her hands the way she did the first two times. A ray of light seemed to penetrate the earth and we saw a great sea of fire, and in that fire there were souls, like black embers floating in the wind. There were great clouds of smoke, and showering sparks everywhere, with shrieks and groans of sorrow and despair that horrified us and made us tremble with fear.

"The devils looked like strange animals, terrible and disgusting, with the transparency of glowing coals. Frightened and begging for help, we raised our eyes to the Lady, who said to us with sadness but also great kindness, 'You saw hell, where the souls of poor sinners go. To save them God wants the world to turn to Me. If they do what I tell you, many souls will be saved and there will be peace.' "

After that came the Second Secret. "The war is going to end. But if people do not stop offending God, another even more terrible war will begin in the reign of Pius XI. If you see the sky lit up by an unknown light, you'll know it's the sign given to you by God, and that he is about to punish the world for its crimes, by war, hunger, and persecutions against the Church and the pope.

"To prevent this I will come to ask for the consecration of Russia to My Immaculate Heart. If they listen to me, Russia will convert and there will be peace; if not, Russia will spread her mistakes throughout the world, starting wars and persecuting the Church. The good will be killed. The pope will suffer, and nations will be destroyed.

"In the end I will triumph. The pope will bless Russia and she will convert and a period of peace will be granted to the world."

For eighty years, we did not know what she revealed to Lúcia and Jacinta after that. The Third Secret of Fatima was perhaps the most closely guarded secret of the Church. Lúcia respected the wish of the Madonna, who said, "Do not tell anybody about it. You may tell Francisco, though."

After they were told the mysterious Third Secret, minutes of uneasy silence followed, during which the children felt overwhelmed, after all they had been shown and told. Finally Lúcia asked in a low voice, "Do you want anything more from me?"

"No, I want nothing more from you today," replied the Lady as she rose up slowly and moved to the east, before disappearing into the sky a great distance away.

Ti Marto described later what everyone there experienced at that moment. "We heard a loud clap of thunder and the little wooden arch, which had two lanterns hanging on it, trembled as if there had been an earthquake. Lúcia, who was still kneeling, sprang up quickly, pointed to the sky, and cried, 'There She goes! There She goes!'

"After a few moments she said, 'Now you can't see her anymore.' This was enough proof for me."

After a few moments of respectful silence everyone

crowded around the children, throwing questions at them. The thoughts of the children seemed far away, and they were terribly shaken. They now knew what kinds of disasters were coming to the world, but they had to keep this knowledge to themselves.

"It's a secret," replied Lúcia, when asked about the message. The people wanted to know if it was a good secret.

"For some it is good, for others it is bad," she answered. She wasn't supposed to say more, and she didn't want to. A photograph taken immediately after the vision shows the anxiety on the faces of the children, who had just seen a symbolic vision of hell.

They had also been told about the real hell that would happen on earth during the twentieth century—the hell of Communist revolutions and the Spanish Civil War, of the Nazi terror and the Second World War, with the Cold War following it; of the arms race and the nuclear threat, and the spread of atheism. This vision put an end to the childhood innocence of Lúcia, Jacinta, and Francisco. Gone forever were their days of carefree play and laughter. Their lighthearted games gave way to serious reflections, along with a deep sadness, and their thoughts now centered on the message they had received from the Lady.

Again and again they remembered the dreadful pictures of hell they had seen. They tried making sacrifices in their lives, sometimes giving away their food to the needy and going hungry all day, or not drinking water, in spite of the heat of summer.

There was another problem for the children to face. More and more curious people came to the village to see them, touch them, and ask them questions. The farmers' fields were overrun by the people and their donkeys, the grain trampled down, and the harvest destroyed. Soon it became impossible for the children to take their sheep out to graze, for they were continually visited by pilgrims. Lúcia's family was forced to sell their flock at a low price. Because of all this Lúcia's mother was angry with her, and punished her almost daily. In addition, she felt the hostility of their neighbors, particularly from the women of the village. The situation was becoming unbearable.

The papers reported on the incidents at the Cova da Íria and the liberal press, which was the voice of the revolutionary government, said that the whole thing was a fraud set up by priests—especially the hated Jesuits—who wanted to gain support for Catholic superstitions.

The bitterest enemy of the apparitions was Artur Santos, the administrator of the province of Villa Nova da Ourém, to which Fatima belonged. His deep hatred for the monarchy and the church had led him to become the editor of the local republican paper. When the new republic started looking for trustworthy people to run their administration, Santos was their man for Ourém. Soon he became the most prominent, most influential, and most feared person in the province.

For Santos, Fatima represented an attack against the rationalist worldview, the republic, and everything that he stood for. It was his business to keep order in the province and to see that the aims of the republic were firmly established and the superstitious Catholic religion eradicated. The last thing he needed was a miracle. He had to crush the superstition of Fatima.

On August 10, 1917, three days before the fourth appearance of the Mother of God, a summons was delivered: the fathers of Lúcia, Jacinta, and Francisco were to appear at the town hall of Ourém on the next day, at eleven o'clock in the morning. Lúcia accompanied her father when he went to the provincial capital, but Ti Marto decided not to take Jacinta and Francisco with him.

"Where is the other child?" roared Santos when he saw Ti Marto there alone, apparently not realizing that three children were involved. He then turned to Lúcia and said, "You! You know the secret. Come on, tell me what it is!" But neither his threats nor his promises had any effect on her, and he could not get her to promise not to visit the Cova again.

In exasperation he finally sent them all home, where Jacinta and Francisco were glad to see that Lúcia was still all right, for they had been afraid she might have been imprisoned, or even executed.

In the early hours of August 13 Fatima was again filled with pilgrims. At least fifteen thousand, perhaps twenty thousand, pilgrims arrived by every type of transportation, from donkeys to automobiles. Never before had the area seen such huge crowds. The homes of the three children were overrun. Hundreds of people wanted them to ask the Madonna to solve their problems. Others flooded them with questions, without giving them a chance to answer, and still others just wanted to touch them. The children were handed from one person to another, to the point where they might have been crushed to death.

Suddenly the children heard their parents calling them. When Lúcia finally managed to fight her way through the crowd and get to her house, Jacinta and Francisco were already there, with Santos in front of them. Once more he tried to get the children to tell him the secret, and when that failed, he tried to make them promise never to go to the Cova again. Then Santos suddenly changed his tone of voice and spoke in a very friendly fashion, saying, "All right, show me that vision of yours, I have to see it to believe it. I'm just like Saint Thomas. Let's go! It will be faster if we take my carriage—no one will bother us on the way."

The children didn't trust this sudden change of heart, and said they would rather go on foot.

"But I must first bring them to Father Ferreira!" said Santos to the parents, who then ordered the children to get inside his carriage. They felt they could not go against the combined authority of the parish priest and the administrator of the province.

They drove to the rectory. Santos sent Lúcia in and waited outside with the other two children and both fathers. Father Ferreira asked Lúcia, "Who teaches you to say the things you talk about?"

"The Lady I saw at the Cova da Íria!"

"People who spread lies, like you do, will be judged and go to hell. More and more people are being deceived by people like you."

"If people who tell lies will go to hell, then I won't go to hell because I'm telling the truth. I only tell about what I saw and what the Lady told me. And if other people go to see her, they go because they want to. We don't ask them to go with us."

"Is it true that the Lady has given you a secret?"

"Yes, but I can't tell you what it is. If you really want to know it, I have to ask the Lady whether I can tell you, and if she gives me permission, I'll tell you what it is."

When the priest wanted to talk to Jacinta and Francisco, Santos interrupted, saying, "That is no longer necessary. They can go, or better still, we can all go together, or it will be too late." The children climbed into Santos's carriage and their fathers followed in a separate carriage.

"The horses fell into a trot and we went to the Cova da Íria," recollected Ti Marto later. "I was relieved, but when we got to the main road, the carriage with the children in it took a sudden turn, the driver whipped the horse, and it bolted like lightning. The whole thing was very cleverly organized." Santos had abducted the children.

"This is not the way to the Cova," said Lúcia in the carriage.

"No, we are driving first to Ourém to visit the priest

there," said Santos. "And if we hurry, we will be back at noon."

After a journey that lasted an hour and a half, the triumphant politician reached his house, led the three children into a little room and told them to wait, then locked the door. He said he would only open the door after they had told him their secret.

"You can kill us, but we don't care," cried out Jacinta defiantly. "That way we'll only get to heaven quicker."

In desperation the children prepared to make their biggest sacrifice, the sacrifice of their lives.

"The administrator has kidnapped the children!" announced someone who had seen what had happened. He spoke to the crowd waiting impatiently at the Cova. A murmur started going around, which became increasingly louder and more excited.

"Let's go to Ourém and protest," someone called out.

"We'll beat them up!" roared another.

"We'll start with the priest," cried a third. "Then we'll finish off the administrator afterward!"

At this moment a clap of thunder interrupted them. People in the crowd winced and some cried out in fear.

"They all backed away from the tree," wrote Maria Carreira later. "The thunder was followed by a flash of lightning; then we saw a small cloud, very white and delicate. It rested on the tree for a moment and then rose and disappeared.

"When we looked around, we all saw the same thing, which happened again during the following months. Our faces reflected the colors of the rainbow: pink, red, and blue. The trees looked as if they had blossoms instead of leaves, as if each leaf had turned into a flower. The earth shone in all colors and so did the clouds; the lanterns on the arch looked as if they were made of pure gold. Our Dear Lady had come, that was certain, although She had not found the children there. As soon as this sign came to an end, everyone went off to Fatima. They protested and rioted against the administrator and the priest, and against everyone they believed had had something to do with the abduction of the children."

The anger of the people was so great that Father Manuel Marques Ferreira put up a notice the next day in which he defended himself against the accusation that he had played a part in the abduction. "I refute this malicious slander. I declare before the whole world that I had nothing to do either directly or indirectly with this outrageous act. The administrator of the district did not tell me about his intentions. Thousands of witnesses can testify that the presence of the children was not essential for the Queen of the Heavens to reveal herself. From now on it is not just three children but thousands of people, of every age, from all walks of life and all classes of society, who have seen all these things with their own eyes."

Was the priest a hypocrite, or had Saul turned into Paul in the face of this indisputable vision of the supernatural?

Meanwhile Santos tried to bribe the children to reveal their secret to him. He then threatened to throw them into

kettles filled with boiling oil. For two hours they sat in a
cell at the local prison, fearing for their lives. Finally he
told the prison warden to bring Jacinta to him.

"You stubborn farmer's brat! I am giving you one last
chance to reveal your secret. The oil is boiling already."
But the brave girl was ready to accept her fate.

"Good, then take her and throw her into the oil!" he
ordered. A grim-faced warden grabbed her and took her
into another room, as Jacinta prayed desperately.

Then it was Francisco's turn. When the warden went
to get him, he found Francisco praying for his sister.
"She's already fried!" said Santos. "Now you'll be next,
so out with the secret!"

"I can't, sir, I can't tell you!"

"You can't? Warden, take him to the same place you
took his sister!"

When he saw his sister was still alive, he embraced
her in relief. The same thing happened with Lúcia. Finally Santos had to accept the fact that nothing he did
was going to get the secret out of the children. He was
defeated. On August 15 he loaded them back into his carriage and brought them to Father Ferreira at the rectory at
Fatima.

A few days later the Madonna appeared to the children, again above an oak tree, but this time near the field
of Valinhos near Aljustral.

Once more the Lady said, "I want you to come on the
thirteenth to the Cova and you must continue to pray the
Rosary daily. During the last month I will perform a

miracle, so that everyone can believe. If you hadn't been taken out of town, the last vision would have been greater."

Lúcia asked her what she should do with all the donations of money that the pilgrims had brought with them to the Cova. The money was now in the safekeeping of Maria Carreira. The Lady told them the money should be put aside for the time being. It was later used to build a chapel at the sight of the visions.

Once more Lúcia begged for the healing of certain sick people.

"Yes, I will cure some during the year. Pray often and make sacrifices for sinners."

After that she rose up and disappeared in the east.

CHAPTER FIVE
DOUBTS AND PROMISES

WHILE LÚCIA, JACINTA, and Francisco were seeing the Lady near Valinhos, people at Aljustrel noticed some remarkable atmospheric phenomena of the kind described by visitors to the Cova. The air cooled down remarkably, and the sun turned various colors. Lúcia's sister Theresa and her husband were among the witnesses.

" 'What is that?' I asked my husband, when I saw the colors reflected on his white shirt," she recalled later.

" 'I think we're all going mad—what do you think?' he replied.

" 'Don't you see?' I said. 'It's just like what happened on the thirteenth.' By the time we arrived at church, the colors had disappeared. Later on we learned that we saw these colors at exactly the same moment the children had their vision at Valinhos."

After the Madonna disappeared, the children broke off the branch that had been touched by her cloak. Lúcia's sister Maria dos Anjos recalled, "Jacinta rushed over to my mother and said, 'Aunty! We saw Our Dear Lady again at Valinhos.'

" 'Jacinta,' my mother replied, 'when are these lies going to stop? Now you've started seeing the Dear Lady wherever you go!'

" 'But we saw her,' and pointing to the branch, she said, 'Look, Aunty, Our Dear Lady stood on this!'

" 'Let me see, let me see,' said Mama. When Jacinta handed her the branch, she smelled it and said, 'What kind of smell is this? It is not spicy, not the smell of roses—it's nothing I recognize, but it's a very fine perfume.' "

From that moment Maria Rosa's skepticism toward the visions changed completely. Suddenly she felt that her daughter hadn't lied to her after all. Lúcia's suffering came to an end. Now, if she was teased by others, it was her mother who defended her, saying, "When all is said and done, it could be true after all."

When Jacinta's father, Ti Marto, came home that evening, the whole house was filled with the fragrance from the branch the children had brought home. "It is the branch on which Our Dear Lady stood," Jacinta explained to him.

The children took very seriously the Lady's request that they make sacrifices. They often refused drinking water, despite the intense heat of August, stopped eating the fruit that well-meaning pilgrims brought them, and they tied strings around various parts of their bodies so tightly that they hurt.

On the evening of September 12 what seemed like an endless stream of pilgrims started pouring into the Cova da Íria, to witness the appearance expected the next day. Although the nights had turned cooler, most of the pilgrims decided to camp in the open, because of the shortage of places to stay in Fatima. Between twenty-five and thirty thousand people were there, most of them immersed in prayer, waiting for the arrival of the children. The three children had a hard time getting through the crowds in order to arrive at the oak tree in time. Vehicles blocked the roads to the Cova, and the whole area looked like a temporary campground.

"The roads were full of people, and all of them wanted to see us and speak to us," Lúcia said later. "There were no differences between the people there. Even wealthy ladies and gentlemen fought their way through the crowds, fell on their knees before us, and begged us to tell their wishes to Our Dear Lady."

Others, who could not reach the children, shouted out requests like "For the love of God, beg Our Lady to cure my crippled son," or "May she heal my blind child!" or "Please, may she bring my husband and my son back home alive from the war!"

All the suffering and misery of mankind seemed to have gathered together at Aljustral. Lúcia was reminded of the biblical scenes of crowds thronging around Jesus, hoping to be helped and healed by him. Some had climbed up onto walls or trees just to see them. Others lifted their children onto their shoulders so they could see more clearly.

Luckily, some men there managed to keep back the crowd and clear the way for the children, so that they could reach the Cova on time.

A deeply moving scene awaited them there. "It was a bigger demonstration of faith than I have ever seen before in my life," recalled a witness later. At the place where the vision was expected to appear, all the men had taken off their hats. Most of the people were kneeling and praying.

Lúcia said, "We finally arrived at the oak tree at the Cova and began to pray the rosary along with the other people there. Soon after that we saw the flash of light and then we saw Our Dear Lady above the oak.

" 'Continue to pray the rosary to end the war. God is pleased with your sacrifices, but He does not want you to sleep tied with the strings; wear them only during the day.'

"I said to her, 'People have asked me to ask you for many things, for the cures of some sick people, and the healing of a deaf-mute.'

" 'Yes, I will cure some but not all. In October I will perform a miracle for everyone to see.' And rising, she disappeared in the same way as before."

Among the pilgrims, made up of both the curious and believers, was a high official of the church, Monsignor João Wuaresma. He had come with a fellow priest to get a firsthand impression of what was happening at the Cova. He described what he experienced. "On a beautiful September morning we left Leiria and drove in a shaky carriage drawn by an old horse to the place where the appearances were said to take place. Pastor Gois found us a place to stand above the Cova, where we could observe what happened without getting too close to where the children were waiting.

"Toward noon there was total silence, except for the murmur of prayers. Suddenly there were shouts of joy and voices praising the blessed Virgin. Arms were raised and fingers pointed toward a certain spot in the sky.

" 'Look, do you see it?' 'Yes, yes, yes!' There was not a single cloud to be seen in the deep blue sky. I raised my eyes and scanned the heavens to see if I could spot something, which those who were luckier than me had already seen, or believed they had seen.

"Suddenly, to my great surprise, I clearly saw a shining sphere gliding majestically through the heavens, moving from east to west. My friend also had the good fortune to see this wonderful and unexpected appearance. Suddenly the sphere disappeared and there was only a most unusual light.

"A little girl was standing near us, dressed very much like Lúcia, and of about the same age. She kept crying out joyfully, 'I still see it! I still see it!' And then, 'Now it's coming down.'

"After a few minutes another child pointed to the sky and called out, 'Now it's going away!' We could see the child following the sphere with her eyes until it disappeared in the direction of the sun.

" 'What did you think of that?' I asked my companion. He was enchanted by what he had seen. 'That was Our Dear Lady,' he answered without any hesitation. That was also my conviction. The children had seen the Mother of God herself, whereas we had only been allowed to see the vehicle that had brought her from heaven.

"I had the impression that all those around us had seen the same thing, for I heard outbursts of joy from many people. But there were some there who were quiet. Near us was a simple and humble woman who wept bitterly, for she had seen nothing at all.

"We felt elated. My friend went from group to group, at the Cova as well as on the road, in order to collect information. The people he spoke to came from all levels of society but they all confirmed the reality of the phenomenon that we, too, had witnessed."

Other witnesses who were closer to the oak tree observed, "A beautiful cloud of smoke formed itself around the wooden arch and rose up slowly, becoming bigger and bigger, and when it was about thirty feet above the ground, it dissolved into the air. This was repeated twice. The three offerings of smoke lasted for about twelve minutes, just as long as the vision itself."

Some who were there claimed to have seen a mysterious rain of rose petals, which fluttered down over the area, but disappeared as soon as they fell to earth. Each of these signs was seen by a large number of people, but no one saw them all. Interestingly enough, they were seen not only by the deeply faithful, but also by skeptics. And yet, all this was only a prelude to the great wonder of October 13, which the Madonna had promised.

At Aljustrel everything was leading up to the great finale. More and more groups of pilgrims visited the hamlet, sought out the children, and asked them the same questions again and again—something the children accepted as one of the trials they had to endure. But one visitor succeeded in winning their confidence. This was the priest Dr. Manuel Formigao, a professor at the Lyceum in Lisbon.

He, too, had been at the Cova on September 13, but had noticed nothing except a darkening of the sun. Because of the crowd he had not been able to get close enough to the actual site to see more.

His experience had not convinced him completely, and only a personal meeting with the three children would make him feel certain that there was indeed something behind the miracle. On September 27 he had long, separate interviews with each of them, and thanks to his records, we have an accurate report of what happened, free of distortion.

The first to be interviewed was Francisco. "What did you see at the Cova during the last few months?" Father Formigao asked.

"I saw Our Dear Lady."

"Where does she appear?"

"On an oak tree."

"Does she appear suddenly or do you see her coming from somewhere else?"

"I see her coming from the direction where the sun rises. And then she stops near the oak."

"Does she come quickly or slowly?"

"She always comes quickly."

"Do you hear what she says? Have you ever spoken to the Lady, and has the Lady ever spoken to you?"

"No, I have never asked her anything and she only speaks to Lúcia."

"Who does she look at? You and Jacinta, or only at Lúcia?"

"She looks at all of us but longer at Lúcia."

"Has she ever wept or smiled?"

"Neither, but she is always very serious."

"How is she dressed?"

"She wears a long dress and a cloak over it, which covers her head and reaches to the hem of her dress."

"What are the colors of the dress and the cloak?"

"White. But the dress has threads of gold in it."

"How is she standing?"

"Like someone who is praying. She holds her hands folded above her waist."

"Does she have anything in her hand?"

"She carries a rosary wound around the palm and the back of her right hand."

"What does she wear on her ears?"

"I can't see her ears—they are covered by the cloak."

"Is the Lady beautiful?"

"Yes, she is beautiful."

"Is she prettier than that girl there?" He pointed to a pretty girl from the village.

"Yes."

"Well, there are women who are lovelier than that girl there."

"She is more beautiful than anyone I have ever seen."

Jacinta was interrogated next. "Have you seen Our Dear Lady, since May, on the thirteenth of every month?"

"Yes."

"Where does she come from?"

"She comes from heaven, from the other side of the sun."

"How is she dressed?"

"She wears a white dress decorated with gold and she wears a cloak, also white, which covers her head."

"What is the color of her hair?"

"I can't see her hair, for it is covered by the cloak."

"Does she wear earrings?"

"I don't know because you can't see her ears."

"How does she hold her hands?"

"Her hands are folded above her waist with the fingers pointing upward."

Lúcia was questioned last. "Is it true that Our Lady has appeared at the place called the Cova da Íria?"

"Yes, that is true."

"How often has she appeared to you?"

"Five times, once each month."

"On which day of the month?"

"Always on the thirteenth, with the exception of August, when I was taken away to Ourém by the mayor. During that month I saw her a few days later, on the nineteenth at Valinhos."

"The people say that Our Dear Lady appeared to you last year as well. Is that true?"

"No, she didn't appear to me last year. In fact, she never came before May this year. I never said anything like that to anybody, for it is not true." (Lúcia didn't tell him about the earlier appearances of the angel.)

"What direction does she come from—the east?"

"I don't know, I don't see her coming from anywhere. I only see her appearing above the oak tree, and when she leaves, she moves in the direction in which the sun rises."

"How long does she stay? For a long or a short time?"

"A short time."

"Long enough to recite the Ave Maria or the Lord's Prayer?"

"She stays longer but the time is not always the same. It is probably not long enough to say all the prayers of the rosary."

"Were you afraid when you saw her for the first time?"

"I was so afraid that I just wanted to run away with Jacinta and Francisco. But she told us not to be afraid, that she would not harm us."

"How was she dressed?"

"She wore a white dress that reached down to her feet. Her head was covered by a cloak of the same color and the same length."

"Have you ever asked her who she is?"

"I asked her but she said she would tell us on October thirteenth."

"Have you asked her where she comes from?"

"Yes, she said she came from heaven."

"When did you ask her this?"

"The second time, on July thirteenth."

"Has she ever smiled? Or did she look sad?"

"She didn't smile, but she wasn't sad either. She always looks very solemn."

"Did she tell you to recite certain prayers?"

"She said that we should recite the rosary in honor of Our Lady of the Rosary so that the world would have peace."

"Did she say that a lot of people should come to the Cova on October thirteenth?"

"No, she didn't say anything like that."

"Is it true that the Lady has told a secret to the three of you, which you are not allowed to tell anybody?"

"Yes."

"Does that apply only to you, or to Jacinta and Francisco as well?"

"No, it's for all three of us."

"Has Our Dear Lady revealed anything more?"

"She said she would perform a miracle on October

thirteenth, so that people will start believing in her appearances."

No wonder, then, that everyone was eagerly waiting for October 13 to see the miracle that the Madonna had promised. But the opposition did not sleep either. On October 13 *Século,* a newspaper with a wide circulation all over the country, published an article ridiculing the events at Fatima, which ended with the prediction that nothing extraordinary would happen on that day.

The cynicism of the outside world did not fail to have its effect, and not even Aljustrel was immune to it. Some people there agreed with the article in the newspaper, awakening fear in the hearts of the families of Lúcia, Jacinta, and Francisco. What would happen if the promised miracle failed to occur? Was there danger that disappointed crowds might become angry and injure the children? Also, a rumor went around that someone was planning to explode a bomb at the site to "put an end to all the nonsense." The situation was becoming critical.

"Won't you finally confess that nothing ever happened at the Cova?" her mother asked Lúcia. She was under so much pressure that she had started doubting again. Lúcia frowned. Before she could answer, Jacinta, who was part of the discussion, interrupted, "Say that if you want, but we have seen her."

Jacinta's defiance strengthened Lúcia's faith and she said, "I am not afraid that I'll be killed. I am absolutely sure that the Lady will do what she has promised."

CHAPTER SIX

THE DANCE OF
THE SUN

AS THE HOUR of the Lady's return drew closer, the crowd became larger. Nearby towns seemed to have been completely depopulated, as if everyone had come to see the vision. People came from Lisbon, and from all parts of the country. Fishermen abandoned their nets, craftsmen left their workshops, farmers their fields, merchants their shops. They all hurried to the Cova da Íria on foot, on horseback, and in wagons, using every possible means of transportation. They pushed their way over the narrow country roads surrounding Fatima, spending the nights under tents or just wrapped up in blankets, undaunted by the weather.

The autumn had colored the leaves red and gold, and a cold wind from the northwest announced the approach of winter. During the night of the twelfth of October there was a continuous drizzle. Hats, coats, shoes, and boots were all soaked with water, and many of the people had worn new clothes to celebrate the occasion. A wet cold pierced them through to their bones. Some people were forced to take off their shoes because they were soaked through.

From luxurious automobiles to carriages with improvised seats, drawn by oxen or mules, all were fighting to make their way through. Many people brought enough food to last for two or even three days. Others brought their pets with them, and there was an incredible din of human voices mixed with braying donkeys, mooing oxen, honking horns, and the ringing of the bells of the carts and cyclists. But the nearer one came to the site of the vision, the more the sounds changed, until finally all you could hear was the loud hum of thousands of people reciting the prayers of the rosary.

Toward dawn on the thirteenth the weather looked threatening. Heavy black clouds gathered over Fatima. At ten o'clock it started raining again and a strong wind whipped water into the faces of the people. Everyone was thoroughly soaked, their wet clothes hanging from their bodies. There were so many visitors that no one could get an accurate count—estimates vary from fifty to seventy thousand. One witness, university professor Dr. Almeida Garrett, gave an estimate of one hundred thousand.

Ti Marto recollected later, "Our house was so full of

people, we couldn't move. Outside there was a cloud-burst and it was raining so hard that you could hardly see anything. The ground was one big mass of mud. My poor wife was totally upset, for the people in the house climbed on everything, from beds and boxes to tables, and got everything dirty. I tried to soothe her by saying, 'The house is so full that nobody else can get in, so at least it can't get worse.'

"When it was time for us to go, and I was just getting ready to leave with the children, a neighbor came up and whispered to me, 'Ti Marto, you'd better not go, because you might be attacked. They wouldn't harm the children, but in your case it's different.'

"I answered, 'No, I'll go, for I have faith. I'm not afraid and I'm confident that everything will end well.'

"Things were different with my poor wife, Olimpia. She was terribly upset. Although she had faith in Our Dear Lady, she was not convinced that everything would go smoothly, for the priest and many other people did not agree with our beliefs about the visions. But the children were absolutely calm and showed no signs of fear.

"Jacinta said to me, 'If the people kill us, we will go to heaven. But the poor people who do that to us, they will go to hell.'

"A lady from Pompalinho came, bringing special clothes for the girls, and helped them get dressed. Lúcia's dress was blue and Jacinta's white. She placed white lace bows on their heads so they looked like little angels as they walked in the procession to the oak tree.

"When we left the house, the rain was streaming down, and the street was full of mud, but that did not prevent the women along the route from kneeling down before the children.

" 'Leave them in peace, dear people,' I called out, for they seemed to think that the children were saints.

"We had a lot of difficulty getting to the Cova and were stopped on the way many times. But we finally arrived. A man picked up my Jacinta and carried her to the arch with the lanterns, clearing a path for them by crying out, 'Make way for the children who see Our Dear Lady!' I ran behind them, and when Jacinta saw me in the crowd, she became frightened and shouted out, 'Please, don't touch my father! Please don't hurt him!'

"The man finally put Jacinta down, but the crowd was still so thick that she began to cry. Lúcia and Francisco managed to get through and join her. My Olimpia was somewhere, I don't know where, but Maria Rosa was nearby.

"Suddenly a man hit me with a stick, and I thought, *Now trouble is about to start.* But nothing happened after that. The people built barriers around me to protect me. When the time came, everything was peaceful."

Maria dos Santos Carreira related later, "A priest was praying near the place where the visions took place. He had spent the whole night there. When the children came at noon, the priest asked them when Our Dear Lady would appear and Lúcia replied, 'At twelve o'clock.'

"The priest looked at his watch and said, 'Look, it's

already twelve. Our Dear Lady does not lie.' After a few minutes he came back to them and said, 'It's long past twelve o'clock. Don't you see, this is all only an illusion. Go away, all of you! Go away!'

"Lúcia refused to move and the priest began to push her backward. Lúcia said to him, with tears in her eyes, 'Anyone who wants to go can go, but I'll stay here. Our Dear Lady said she would come. She came every time before and she will come this time too.'

"A moment later she turned her eyes toward the east and called out, 'Jacinta, kneel down, our Lady is coming! I've seen the flash of light!' The priest said nothing more. I never saw him again."

Lúcia called out to the crowd, "Be quiet! Please be quiet! Our Lady is coming."

The children's faces were transformed, and their expressions became solemn, as they watched the wonderful Lady for the last time together, floating above the oak tree, surrounded by bright light.

"What does Your Grace want from me?" asked Lúcia once again.

"I wish to tell you that I want a chapel built here in my honor. I am the Lady of the Rosary. Continue to pray the rosary every day. The war is going to end and the soldiers will soon return to their homes."

Lúcia said, "I have many things to ask you—if you would cure some sick people and if you would convert some sinners."

"Some yes, others no. They must change their lives

and then ask forgiveness for their sins." She seemed to become sad as she added, "They should stop offending Our Lord, for He is already very angry."

"Do you wish anything more?" Lúcia asked her.

"No, nothing."

"Then I won't ask you for more either."

Then the beautiful Lady left the children for the last time. She opened up her hands and out came a beam of light. She rose up into the heavens and moved toward the sun. The light that came from her seemed to blend with the light of the sun, which had suddenly come out from behind the clouds. Lúcia shouted, "Look, there she goes, there she goes! Look at the sun!"

The rain suddenly stopped. Thousands of umbrellas closed, and everyone looked toward the sun. What they saw took their breath away: it was the miracle that the Lady had promised them. The newspaper *Dia* of October 17, 1917, described it this way: "At about one o'clock in the afternoon it stopped raining. The pearl-gray sky cast a strange light on the landscape. The sun seemed to be covered by a veil, so that you could look at it with bare eyes.

"The clouds formed a ring around the sun, which looked like a disk of mother of pearl. Then its color changed to silver and it began to revolve. A cry of surprise went up from the spectators and all the people fell to their knees. The color of the light changed to a lovely blue, as if the sun was shining through the stained-glass window of a cathedral. Slowly the blue color faded and the people, still kneeling with outstretched hands, were bathed in a yellow light. Their faces, their clothes, everything was colored yellow. The people wept and prayed when they saw what they had come to see. Seconds seemed like hours, the experience was so intense."

Even the newspaper *Século,* which had been so skeptical about Fatima before, had to concede that "a scene right out of the Bible was observed by the astonished crowd, which was standing bareheaded, looking toward the sky. The sun began to tremble and went into movements that defied all laws of nature. It seemed to be dancing—that was the expression used by some of the people who described it. Others said that the sun seemed to be trembling, and some swore that it began to rotate like a huge wheel of fire, then came toward the earth as if it was going to scorch it. Many saw the light of the sun changing colors." This became known as the "miracle of the sun."

Ti Marto said, "We could look directly at the sun without being blinded. It seemed to flicker and throw out beams of light in various directions, covering everything in different colors. The astonishing thing was that it did not hurt our eyes to look at it.

"It was quiet. Then the sun suddenly started dancing and looked as if it was tearing itself away from the heavens and rushing toward us. That was a frightening moment."

Maria dos Santos Carreira said, "The sun bathed us in many colors of light, yellow, blue, white. It seemed to tremble and quake, then it turned into a wheel of fire that looked like it was going to crash down on everyone. The people cried out, 'We're all going to be killed!' Others called out to Our Dear Lady for help, begging forgiveness for their sins. One woman began to confess her sins loudly. At last the sun stopped coming and we breathed a sigh of relief that we were all still alive. The miracle that the children had predicted had taken place."

Dr. Domingo Pinto Coelho, of the magazine *Ordem,* wrote, "The sun was at one moment enveloped in a red flame, then in yellow and then in deep purple, and it seemed to rotate at an unbelievable speed. For a time it looked as if it was leaving the heavens and approaching the earth, accompanied by great heat."

A priest, Manuel Pereira da Solva, wrote the same evening to the vicar of the cathedral, Pereira de Almeida, "The sun seemed to have a clearly defined outline. It rushed down at us and stopped at about the height of the clouds, then started rotating like a ball of fire at a dizzying speed. This lasted for about eight minutes. The atmosphere got dark and all the people seemed to take on a yellow glow. They fell on their knees in the mud."

Another witness, Dona Maria do Carmo da Cruz Menez, said, "Suddenly the rain stopped, and the sun came through. It seemed to shine on everyone. Then it started turning like a wheel of fire, giving off light in all the colors of the rainbow. We were all bathed in these colors. People cried out and many wept. I was deeply impressed and said to myself, 'Dear God, how great is Your might.'"

Alfredo da Silva Santos remembered that "the sun began to move and suddenly seemed to drop down from the sky toward us like a wheel of fire. My wife—we were newly married—fainted. I was so paralyzed with fear that I couldn't do anything to help her. My brother-in-law, João Vassalo, helped her up. I fell on my knees, and forgot everything else."

Perhaps the most interesting and precise description comes from a scientist who was there, Professor Almeida Garrett of the University of Coimbra. He said, "It must have been about 1:30 P.M. when, at the spot where the children were standing, a slender, bluish column of smoke rose to a height of about six feet above their heads and ended about six feet above that. This phenomenon, which I could see clearly, lasted for several seconds. I did not look at my watch and cannot say whether it lasted more or less than a minute. The smoke vanished suddenly, but reappeared later for a second and then a third time. Each time, especially the third time, a clear beam of light went up and disappeared in the gray atmosphere.

"Suddenly I heard cries coming from thousands of people and saw that the crowd had turned away from the oak tree, and were now all looking in the opposite direction, at the sky. The sun, which had been hiding behind dark clouds, broke through and shone brightly. I looked in the same direction and I saw the sun, clearly defined and radiant, but it did not hurt my eyes to look at it.

"I could not agree with the description, which I often heard at Fatima, that the sun looked like a disk of dull silver. The color was more intense, clearer and brighter. It was not in the least like the moon on a clear night. It was not spherical like the moon and it wasn't the same color. It looked like a shining wheel made of mother of pearl. I had the feeling it was a living being. We did not see the sun shining through fog, because there was no fog there at all.

"Descriptions like 'opaque,' 'diffuse,' or 'veiled' do not apply to this disk. It radiated light and heat and had clear contours with a clearly defined border. The sky was covered with bright cirrus clouds through which we could see the blue sky. Clouds were moving from west to east, but they did not darken the light of the sun. They sometimes looked pink or blue as they went past. The remarkable thing is that we could look at this glowing light without any discomfort, except for two occasions, when the sun threw out glowing rays, which caused us to look away. This phenomenon lasted for about ten minutes.

"The sun did not remain in place, but started rotating at a mad speed. Suddenly, cries of fear went up from the crowd. It seemed as if the sun, spinning wildly, had detached itself from the sky and was rushing toward the earth, as if it was going to scorch us with its fire. Those were terrifying moments.

"During this solar phenomenon, which I have tried to describe in detail, the colors of the atmosphere were changing. When I was looking at the sun, I felt that everything around me had become darker. I looked first at objects close to me and then farther off toward the horizon.

"Everything had taken on the color of amethysts. Even the shadow of an oak tree near me had the same color. I was afraid that my retina had been damaged, except in that case I would not have seen everything colored purple. I closed my eyes and covered them with my hands in order to prevent more light from getting in. Then I turned my back toward the sun and opened my eyes. But the landscape still had the same purple hue and it was not a solar eclipse. When I looked toward the sun again, the atmosphere had cleared.

"Shortly after that I heard a farmer near me call out, 'Look, this woman is completely yellow!' And in fact everything around me, both close and far away, looked as if it was made of old yellow damask. All the people looked as if they had jaundice. I still remember how amused I was to see them looking so unattractive. My hands, too, had the same color.

"I experienced the phenomenon that I describe here while in a sane and healthy state of mind, without being under any form of emotional stress or influence. I leave it to others to explain it."

Interestingly enough, the solar miracle was observed not only at Fatima but also twenty-five miles away. A witness, the poet Afonso Lopes Vieira, described it as follows: "On October 13, 1917, I was enchanted by a remarkable spectacle in the skies, which I observed from the veranda of my house. I had never seen anything like that before. At that time I did not know about the predictions of the children."

Twelve miles away a whole school of children was surprised by the phenomenon. Father Inacio Laurenco Pereira, a nine-year-old schoolboy at the time, later recalled, "At about noon we heard cries and calls from children on the street that runs past the school. The teacher ran out first to see what was happening. Outside, children were crying and pointing to the sun. It was a great miracle, and one could see it clearly from the top of the hill where my village was.

"I looked at the sun spellbound. I could see it without hurting my eyes. It looked like a ball of snow that was rotating, then suddenly it seemed to fall toward the earth in a zigzag path. I ran away, frightened, and hid myself among the weeping crowd of people, who were expecting the end of the world to come at any moment. They wept and begged God to forgive their sins.

"We all ran to the two chapels in the village and found them full of people. During these long minutes, when the marvel was taking place, everything around us took on all the colors of the rainbow, one after the other. We saw ourselves in blue, yellow, red, and so on. This only increased the panic. After about ten minutes the sun returned to its place and became dull and lusterless again. When people realized the danger was over, they started rejoicing and thanked and praised Our Dear Lady."

When the people at the Cova da Íria recovered from their fright, they became aware of another phenomenon.

Their clothes, which had been dripping wet from the heavy rains, were now absolutely dry. The warmth that had come from the dancing sun had dried them within minutes. The three little visionaries had seen more than the others. Near the rotating disk of the sun they saw the holy family. To the right was the Virgin in a white robe and a sky-blue cloak, to the left of her Joseph with the child Jesus. They blessed the world with the sign of the cross. After that Jesus appeared by himself, dressed completely in red, and blessed the people.

When the miracle was over, the crowd streamed toward the three children. Everyone was enthusiastic now, wanting to touch them and somehow grab some of the grace that surrounded them. Lúcia's head scarf was pulled away and someone cut off a lock of her hair. Little Jacinta broke out in tears.

"What did the Virgin tell you?" was the question most frequently asked.

"The war will come to an end today, and you can expect the soldiers to return shortly," answered Lúcia and Jacinta, in a naive interpretation of the words of the apparition. The war did not come to an end that day, but went on for another year. Later, when the words of the children were not immediately fulfilled, many people began to have doubts about Fatima.

During the following days reports about the solar miracle of Fatima appeared in newspapers and magazines all over the country. It put a seal of authenticity on the apparitions. Between fifty and a hundred thousand eyewitnesses, among them critics, skeptics, atheists, and representatives of the liberal press, could not all have been victims of mass hysteria. No astronomical observatory, in Portugal or anywhere else in the world, observed any anomaly on the surface of the sun that day. This ruled out any natural explanation.

Today, when we read descriptions of "the dance of the sun," about a rotating silver disk that generated heat and approached the earth, we think immediately of UFOs. But whatever it was that people saw at Fatima, we know one thing: It came from another world.

CHAPTER SEVEN

DEATH OF AN ANGEL

AFTER THE DANCE of the sun, life at Fatima was never the same. News of the events of October 13 had hardly begun to spread, when thousands of people came pouring into the village. These were people who regretted not having been present, but who still hoped to receive some benefit from the event. Especially on Sundays and on the thirteenth of every month, there were long processions of pilgrims praying the rosary as they visited the Cova.

Nothing could stop people from coming to the site, even a vandalism attempt by members of the nearby Freemasons' lodge during the night of October 23, ten days after the miracle of the sun.

"They used an ax to cut down the tree at the place where the three children stood during the famous phenomenon of October 13, which was reported in detail in the press," wrote the newspaper *Diario de Noticias*. "These people then carried away the tree, along with a table that had a simple altar on it. They also removed a wooden arch, two lanterns, and two crucifixes."

The destruction did not stop there. The stolen items were displayed at a house at Santarem, and an admission fee was charged to anyone who wanted to see them. Then they were carried through the town in a mock procession.

The *Século* reported that "two drummers marched in front, and behind them came the tree on which Our Dear Lady appeared. After that came the wooden arch with the burning lanterns, the table, and the objects that the faithful had placed on it, turning it into an improvised altar. Reciting a parody of a prayer, the procession went through the main streets of the town."

Even the reporter of this republican newspaper was shocked by the outrage. He wrote, "The affair was a scandalous disgrace. How could the authorities possibly tolerate such a thing, when, at the same time, they forbid church processions?"

However, the next day, when faithful pilgrims went to the Cova da Íria, they were relieved to find that the wrong tree had been cut down. But the activities of the Masons had not yet ended. They organized a demonstration at the site to distract the pilgrims from their prayers. First, they brought a herd of donkeys that filled the air with braying. After that three men made speeches ridiculing religion. They distributed thousands of leaflets, warning people against the "fatal propaganda" that was a "miserable attempt to push the Portuguese nation back into the darkest period of the past."

But despite all this the number of pilgrims increased and with them came donations for the building of the chapel that the Mother of God had requested.

Maria Carreira volunteered to hold the money in trust, which soon earned her the name "Maria da Capella" (Mary of the Chapel). Soon there was enough to start building, and eventually the chapel was completed. It was difficult, at first, to find a priest for the chapel, since the visions of Fatima had not yet been officially recognized by the Church.

On May 13, 1920, the third anniversary of the vision, the statue of Our Lady of Fatima arrived, which had been sculpted according to descriptions given by the children. The statue was installed and the chapel was consecrated by the local priest. When Lúcia first saw the statue, she bent over it with tears running down her cheeks, as memories rushed through her head. Her heart was troubled, for she was reminded of her two beloved companions, Jacinta and Francisco, who were now dead, exactly as the Lady had foretold.

The visions of the Lady had been the greatest experience of the children's short lives, but the days afterward were filled with suffering. Not only were there the sacrifices they had voluntarily taken on, but there was sickness as well. The once joyful and carefree children had turned into pensive and withdrawn creatures, with only one thought in mind: to fulfill their religious obligations and wait for their eventual journey to heaven.

"I do not want to become anything at all, I just want to die and go to heaven," answered Francisco when a lady asked him whether he wanted to become a priest.

During this period Jacinta had three more visions of the Blessed Virgin, which she told only to Lúcia and her closest relatives. On one occasion she confided in her mother, "I am thinking of the Savior and the Mother of God, of sinners and about the war to come. How many people will die in it! So many houses will be destroyed, so many priests will be killed. Oh, how terrible it all is! If only they would stop insulting and hurting God, this war would not happen."

Since World War I had just come to an end, her mother couldn't have known what she was talking about. But the Second World War was on the horizon.

A year after the visions, in either October or December of 1918 (the record isn't clear), Jacinta, Francisco, and their mother fell ill with the Spanish flu, which was raging through Europe in those days. Soon after that Jacinta had one more vision, about which she said to Lúcia, "Our Dear Lady came to visit us and said she would soon take Francisco with her to heaven. She asked me if I wanted to convert more sinners. I said yes. She then said that I would go to a hospital and suffer a great deal there. I asked her whether you would come with me. She said no, and that is what hurts me the most.

She said my mother would take me to the hospital, and after that I would have to stay there alone."

On April 4, 1919, the first part of this prophecy was fulfilled. Francisco died after a severe inflammation of the lungs. Shortly after that Jacinta's health took a turn for the worse. A two-month-long treatment at the local hospital didn't help, and when her physician, Dr. Formigao, visited her afterward, he was shocked by her condition. "She resembles a skeleton, her arms are frightfully thin," he said. "Since leaving the hospital she has never been free of fever. It is heartbreaking to see her. Tuberculosis is now eating up her weak body."

Sometime in the autumn of 1919 Jacinta confided to Lúcia, "The Madonna has told me that I will be taken to a hospital in Lisbon, and that after that I won't see you or my parents anymore. After much suffering I will die alone. But I shouldn't be afraid, because she will come herself to take me to heaven."

This prophecy, too, was soon fulfilled. In January 1920 a well-known Lisbon doctor came as a pilgrim to Fatima and saw Jacinta in her miserable condition. He insisted that she be taken at once to a hospital in Lisbon. She was sad at having to leave Fatima, but Jacinta accepted her fate.

"Don't tell the Third Secret to anyone, even if they threaten you" were her parting words to Lúcia.

In Lisbon she was brought at first to the orphanage of Our Dear Lady of Miracles. The mother superior, Mother Godinho, soon became her surrogate mother and confidante. On February 2, 1920, Jacinta was taken to the D. Estefania hospital to be treated by the most prominent pediatrician in Lisbon, Dr. Castro Freire.

"It was soon clear to me that a little angel had come into our house," wrote the mother superior, describing the short time she had with Jacinta. "During her stay she must have been visited by Our Dear Lady more than once. I remember her telling me, 'Please, dear Mother, leave me alone for a bit, I am waiting for Our Dear Lady.' Just after that her face took on a radiant expression. Sometimes a ball of light was seen nearby, like the one at Fatima."

She carefully noted down everything Jacinta said after these appearances. "If men do not change their ways," Jacinta said once, "Our Lady will send the world a worse punishment than it has ever seen. It will first happen to Spain." With that Jacinta predicted the Spanish Civil War, which started in 1936 and preceded the Second World War. Once Jacinta mentioned "the terrible events that will happen around 1940," referring to the Second World War.

Another time she said, "Our Dear Lady wants my two sisters to enter a cloister. But since my mother will not allow this, she will take them both to heaven soon." This prophecy was also fulfilled. Soon after Jacinta's death her two sisters Florinda and Teresa also died, at the ages of seventeen and sixteen.

Toward the end of February 1920, shortly after Jacinta's death, Mother Godinho told all her statements to Dr. Manuel Formigao, which he published in 1927 in his book *The Great Miracle of Fatima*.

The messages of the Madonna and the secrets revealed to the children in 1917 were written down by Lúcia much later, so Jacinta's statements are the earliest evidence that the prophecies of the Lady were genuine. However, one of the things the girl predicted did not happen. "Our Lord is angry at the sins and crimes in Portugal. For this reason there's a terrible danger coming, especially to the city of Lisbon. It seems that a civil war will break out, with killings, fires, and destruction of all kinds. Everyone who can should run away." But civil war broke out in Spain, not in Portugal. However, she also emphasized that this could be avoided if people changed their ways. Perhaps the reawakening of religious life that was going on there, despite the efforts of the secular government, prevented these catastrophes from happening. We will never know.

On April 25, 1954, shortly before her death, Mother Godinho wrote a long letter to Pope Pius XII in which she asked that her institution be officially designated as a convent. In that letter she revealed details about her conversations with Jacinta, which included the following warning: "Prepare yourself for the year 1972, when sins will cause much pain to the pope."

In fact, Pope Paul VI declared on June 29, 1972, "It seems as if the smoke of Satan has found its way into the temple of God somehow. We believe that something is trying to create division and destroy the achievements of the Ecumenical Council." We don't know if he knew about Jacinta's statement, or what incident within the Vatican led him to make this statement. Still, this statement by the pope confirmed the prediction of Jacinta.

Mother Godinho recalled another of Jacinta's sayings. "She said that 'the triumph of Our Lord hasn't come yet, but first there will be many tears, because His will is not being respected in the world.' And she told me she was upset because she didn't know how to say this clearly, but she wanted to try anyway. 'There is a secret in heaven and another one on the earth, and the second one is frightening. It already seems like the end of the world, and during this time everything will be separated from heaven, which will become as white as snow.' "

On February 10 Dr. Castro Freire operated on Jacinta. Shortly after that she had her last vision. When the Mother Superior visited her at the hospital, Jacinta told her, "I feel better now. Our Dear Lady said she would soon relieve me of my pain and take me to heaven." On February 20, 1920, Jacinta died. Her body was taken by Mother Godinho to Vila Nova de Ourém. There she was dressed in a white communion dress with a blue sash, put into a coffin, and laid to rest in the burial vault of a noble family, which regarded her as their little guardian angel.

On September 12, 1934, the remains of Jacinta and Francisco were reburied in a grave chosen especially for them at the cemetery of Fatima. When they opened Jacinta's coffin, they found that her body, although wasted by so much illness, showed no signs of decay or decomposition. After the beautiful basilica was built at the site of the vision, the bodies were transferred there in 1951 and buried inside the church, close to the altar.

Fate had other plans for Lúcia. She was to become a nun. On June 17, 1921, she entered the college of the order of Saint Dorothy at Asilo de Vilar and was accepted into the order on October 24, 1925. Her new home was the convent of Tui in Spain, near the Portuguese border. She became a novice on October 2, 1926, and finally took her permanent vows on October 3, 1934.

She took this step because of the religious feelings that had been awakened by the visions, but her steps were guided by Church authorities, who at that time were investigating the incidents at Fatima. They wanted to have her under their control, so they could control the cult of Fatima itself. Besides the actual site of the visions Lúcia's house at Aljustrel was the main destination for thousands of pilgrims. After her departure attention was diverted to the chapel at the Cova, where the basilica was built later. There, all religious proclamations were made by priests who were appointed by the Church.

Personal cults, even if they are inspired by deep devotion, are not encouraged by the Church, for fear that they may get out of hand and go against Catholic dogma. The traditional teachings of the Church must always be at the center of any revelation. Even saints are honored only after their deaths and after careful investigation by the Church.

One year after the apparitions, in 1918, the diocese of

Leiria, to which Fatima belongs, received a new bishop. Don José Alves Correira da Silva, who had been tortured and crippled in the prisons of the republicans, was installed there. His first official act was to remove Lúcia from her home in Aljustrel and start a thorough investigation of the events.

"It would be best for all concerned," the bishop stated, "to send the girl to live as a student at a school far away from Fatima." He chose a place where no one knew her or would recognize her. Maria Rosa, Lúcia's mother, brought her personally to the bishop's residence at Leiria and agreed to his suggestion.

"You should tell no one where you are going," the bishop told Lúcia.

"No, sir, I won't," she answered timidly.

"At the school you must tell no one who you are."

"No, sir, I won't."

"You should not talk about the apparitions at Fatima anymore."

"No, sir," answered Lúcia, in a soft voice. She left for an unknown future. It was now up to others to preserve the message of Fatima.

The dance of the sun, witnessed by between fifty and one hundred thousand people, was a marvel that could not be disputed. But the greatest miracle, at least for the Church, was known as the Fatima Effect, which was the renewal of faith in Portugal, the country where, only a few years before, the government had tried to stamp out religion.

But the republicans fought back, and declared war on this miracle. On May 13, 1920, a huge pilgrimage to the installation of the statue of Our Lady was organized, on the third anniversary of the first apparition. This alarmed the government. The secretary of the interior wrote to the district administrator of Vila Nova de Ourém, ordering him to take measures against what he called "this shameless Jesuit trick."

This led to an emergency meeting at the town hall. Administrator Artur Santos decided to ask for military help from Santarém. On the morning of May 13 all incoming traffic to Ourém was blocked, and a squadron of republican soldiers galloped off toward Fatima. Infantry and cavalry cordoned off the road leading to the Cova da Íria. Only those who had arrived at the Cova during the previous evening, or very early in the morning, were allowed to stay. The pilgrims who came later did not get to visit the statue.

Although the procession did not take place, the statue was installed anyway. Santos told the mayor of Fatima that, in the future, processions could be held only with his permission. "Keep me informed personally about every incident of a superstitious nature that occurs in connection with the so-called Miracle of Fatima," he said.

When the threats against the "Fatima cult" became greater, Maria da Capella removed the statue from the chapel and took it to her house for safety. She brought it to the chapel only on feast days. Her worst fears were soon confirmed. On March 6, 1921, members of the local Freemasons' lodge set off four explosive charges, which had been placed in the chapel. The roof of the chapel was completely destroyed, and it was some time before the bishop finally gave permission for it to be restored. A fifth bomb, attached to the oak on which the Mother of God had appeared, failed to explode, and this was considered a miracle by many believers.

Regarding the statue itself, Lúcia commented later, "I was rather disappointed when I saw it. To start with, she looks too happy, as if free of care. When I saw Our Lady, she looked sad and full of pity. But in any case, it is impossible to make a statue which can be even remotely as beautiful as she is."

CHAPTER EIGHT

THE MIRACLE
OF FATIMA

EARLY IN THE morning of June 17, 1921, Lúcia knocked at the door of the school of Asilo de Vilar. She was accompanied by a nun, who had been appointed by the bishop to look after her. It was cool, and dawn was just breaking through. The bells of the cloister's chapel were ringing for early mass.

The heavy oak door opened and a sister hastily invited them in and led them to the chapel. When the mass was over, Lúcia was taken to the sacristy and was presented before the priest and the mother superior, Mother Maria das Dores Magalhães. The resolute lady took a long look at the troubled but intelligent face of the fourteen-year-old country girl. "She is a wild animal," she said, "but we'll tame her."

She repeated what the bishop said, that Lúcia was to

keep her real identity secret. "If people ask you for your name, you will reply, 'My name is Maria das Dores.' "

"Yes, Mother."

"When they ask you where you come from, you will say, 'From the neighborhood of Lisbon.' "

"Yes, Mother."

"You will never talk to anybody about the events at Fatima."

"Yes, Mother."

"You will ask no questions and give no answers."

"Yes, Mother."

"You will not go for walks with any of the other girls, and you will not tell them why, even if they ask you. Do you understand?"

"Yes, Mother."

It was the hardest period of Lúcia's young life. For the first time she was completely separated from her family, her home, and her past. From that day on her life consisted only of prayer and study. She was allowed to write to her mother only on rare occasions, and the letters were strictly censored by the mother superior. All news about Fatima was deliberately withheld from her.

Lúcia was a boarding pupil and was treated the same as everyone else. She suffered under the apparent coldness of her teachers. But she learned a lot: reading, writing, and even typing; and sewing and embroidery, which soon became her passion. After only a year she was capable of writing an essay on the events of 1917. But before she did this, she had to ask for permission.

She was finally given the permission she needed, and discovered her writing talent for the first time, a talent that would develop more in the future, although at the time she said, "I write so badly but I can't do any better, I am still a student."

When a photograph of the undecayed body of Jacinta was sent to her years later, in 1935, she described her memories of her cousin in a letter to Bishop da Silva that was so full of colorful details that the bishop asked her to write down everything she remembered about Jacinta. The result was so impressive that he asked her to write more details about the events at Fatima. The first four volumes, finished in 1941, contain all the details about the visions and the messages of the Mother of God, word for word as Lúcia recalled them. She could visualize everything that had happened and later explained that she could do this because "these magical things, when we see or hear them, impress themselves so deeply on our souls that is impossible to forget them. Unless God deliberately wants us to forget, they will remain in our memories forever."

The beatification of the Carmelite nun Saint Theresa, on April 29, 1923, was an important topic of discussion at Lúcia's school. This mystic, who died at the age of twenty-five, wrote a book titled *History of a Soul,* which became one of the most popular religious books of that time. She was a model for many Catholic girls, and Lúcia decided she wanted to become a Carmelite nun too.

"You will never be able to stand the strict discipline

of that order," said the mother superior discouragingly. "You'd better choose a less strict one." So Lúcia chose the order of the Sisters of Saint Dorothy, and was sent as a postulant to Tui in Spain. On October 24, 1925, Lúcia left the school in the company of one of the nuns from the school. She was heartily welcomed at the convent, and it was there that she realized the messages of Fatima had not come to an end after all.

After dinner on the evening of December 10, 1925, Lúcia retired to her bare cell to pray, as usual. She knelt down with her rosary and recited the Lord's Prayer, followed by the first Ave Marias, as she let the beads roll through her fingers. In the middle of her prayers she looked up and saw Her once again. The Mother of God stood on a radiant cloud, with the boy Jesus at her side. Lúcia could hardly breathe, she was so filled with joy.

The Lady said to her, "Tell the world that I promise to be there, at the moment of death, with all those who, on the first Saturdays of five months in a row, confess and receive Holy Communion. They must recite five decades of the Rosary and keep me company for fifteen minutes while meditating on the mysteries of the Rosary." She had hardly finished speaking these words, when the entire apparition vanished.

Lúcia told Mother Magalhães and the priest who was her confessor about this vision. The priest asked her to write it all down, while the mother superior informed Bishop da Silva. Lúcia also wrote to her confessor at home, who asked her for a detailed report, which luckily still exists.

On February 15, 1926, Lúcia had another vision. She had just gone out into the garden of the convent to empty the trash, when she noticed a young boy standing there. She spoke to him and asked him whether he had come to pray, but he replied, "Have you told the world what the Heavenly Mother asked you to?" and turned into the boy Jesus of her vision.

She told him how difficult it was for her to tell even the people close to her about the visions. He replied, "It is all right if your superiors announce it, so that people will believe it, even if they don't know it was you who had the revelation."

Meanwhile, the official organization of the Church was becoming more and more convinced that the visions of Fatima were genuine. On May 3, 1922, the bishop of Leiria wrote a pastoral letter in which he declared, "We have interrogated the last seer [Lúcia] in various ways. Her reports and answers are simple and genuine. We can find nothing in them that is immoral or contrary to the faith.

"We ask ourselves, how can this girl, now fourteen years old, have the kind of influence on people that explains the stream of pilgrims to Fatima? How can her personal appearance attract such crowds? It is unlikely that something like this would happen, since we are dealing with a child who had only the simplest upbringing and no education whatsoever."

Eight years later, in October 1930, the bishop published a second pastoral letter describing the results of his investigation of Fatima and proclaiming the following:

1. We declare the visions of the shepherd children at the Cova da Íria, parish of Fatima, from May 13 to October 13, 1917, to be worthy of belief.
2. We officially permit the worship of Our Lady of Fatima.

From that moment on Fatima was not just a village in the Serra de Aire, but a center of Christian belief in a time of hardship. Pilgrims came there by the hundreds of thousands, not only from Portugal, but from all over the world. During one of the darkest periods in the history of mankind, when Fascism was ruling Germany and Italy and a civil war was raging in the neighboring country of Spain, Portugal, the land of the Virgin Mary, was a peaceful island surrounded by chaos and destruction.

Meanwhile, the Fatima visions were confirmed by further miracles. On May 13, 1924, over two hundred thousand pilgrims gathered at the Cova to celebrate the seventh anniversary of the apparitions, when a mysterious rain of flower petals once more fell on the congregation. This time the phenomenon was even photographed. A witness described it this way: "Higher up they were big, but as they came nearer they became smaller and smaller and then finally disappeared. Men held out their hands to catch them but, when they looked, found nothing in them." The most prominent witness was Bishop da Silva himself.

Soon the first healings began. Maria da Capella reported, "From everywhere people came here with their sufferings and misery. During the Spanish flu epidemic thousands came here, praying and begging for relief. They were heard, for from that day onward no one else in this district fell victim to the disease. After that, worship of the Lady of Fatima increased even more, and after the chapel was built, thousands of people came here."

To provide water for the pilgrims a well was dug at the site in 1926. The water at first flowed out slowly, but then bubbled out in a strong stream. The pilgrims started believing that the water had healing powers. They filled bottles and jugs, bathed wounds with it, and drank the muddy liquid, trusting implicitly that the miraculous power of the place was stronger than the laws of hygiene.

As a witness, José Alves, reported later, "Never before had so many miracles happened as they did then. I saw people with sore legs and open wounds, who washed their legs with that water and then could throw away their bandages, for Our Lady had healed them. Others knelt down and drank the water and were healed of their sickness."

This only provoked the hostility of the opponents of Fatima. On July 15, 1927, the district administrator of Ourém decided to intervene, "owing to the acute public health danger." Together with a representative of the

Department of Health, he went to the Cova da Íria to inspect the well and decided that the conditions there were "disgusting." He ordered it filled in immediately. But his instructions were ignored, and the well still exists today.

For those who believed in the apparitions of Fatima, the fate of the Portuguese nation was the real miracle, a shining example to show the world that it could be saved if it would only open itself to the life of the spirit.

Father Michel de la Sainte Trinité, author of one of the most detailed studies of Fatima, wrote, "After seven years of violent and fanatical persecution, after religion had been banished from public life for a century, the Church, as if by a miracle, suddenly won back all its rights."

On December 5, 1917, the commander of the army, Sidonio Pais, staged a coup against "the demagogy of democrats," as he called it. Three days later he disbanded the parliament and was appointed president of the Republic, with dictatorial powers. A day later he lifted all sanctions against the bishops, who were then allowed to return to their dioceses. All laws separating the Church and the state were declared invalid. In June he established official diplomatic relations with the Vatican.

The republicans and Freemasons declared open war against him. On December 14, 1918, Pais, who had just attended mass, was assassinated at the railway station in Lisbon. A military revolt followed, on May 28, 1926, led by General Gomes de Costa. Supported by the Church, big landholders, and the army, the military disbanded the parliament once more and suspended the constitution. Shortly afterward Antonio de Oliveira Salazar was appointed finance minister, with almost unlimited powers. On July 5, 1932, he was named prime minister and remained head of the government for thirty-six years, until 1968. A new constitution gave him dictatorial powers.

When the civil war broke out in the neighboring country of Spain, he supported General Francisco Franco, who, like himself, was conservative, Catholic, and militaristic. Because of him Portugal was at least saved from Communism. Of the two alternatives military dictatorship may have been the lesser evil. After the deaths of Franco and Salazar both Spain and Portugal became democracies without further bloodshed. Without the religious belief that was rekindled by the Fatima apparitions, Communist revolutionaries might have taken over these countries, as they did so many others.

On June 13, 1929, Lúcia went to the chapel of the convent of Saint Dorothy to pray before the altar, as she did every Thursday at eleven. But when she arrived this time, she had a vision. "I prayed every Thursday night during the holy hour from eleven P.M. to midnight," Lúcia wrote later. "One night, when I was alone, I stretched out on the floor to say my prayers. After a while I felt tired, so I stood up and prayed some more. The only light in the chapel came from the lamp.

"Suddenly the entire chapel was filled with a supernatural light, and above the altar there appeared a cross of light that reached up to the ceiling. In a bright glow of light near the top of the cross, I saw the torso of a man, with a dove of light on his chest. Under that, nailed to the cross, was the torso of another man. Somewhat below this second man I saw, floating in the air, a chalice and a large host, from which drops of blood were falling, coming from the face and a wound in the chest of the crucified man. The blood ran over the host and fell into the chalice." This was similar to the visions of the angel that Lúcia had had before she first saw the Lady with Jacinta and Francisco.

She continued, "Our Lady stood under the right arm of the cross, and under the left arm of the cross there appeared big letters, that looked like they were made of water. They fell onto the altar, forming the words *Grace and mercy.* I realized I had been shown the mystery of the Holy Trinity and I received an inner understanding about it that I cannot reveal.

"Our Lady then said to me, 'The moment has come when God wants the pope to dedicate Russia to Me, promising to save it this way. Sacrifice yourself for this, and pray.'"

On May 29, 1930, Lúcia wrote to her confessor, "If I am not mistaken, God promises to put an end to the persecution in Russia if the pope will perform a solemn and public act that will consecrate Russia to the devotion of Mary, and if all the bishops of the world will do the same."

Through her confessor and the bishop of Leiria, Lúcia told the Madonna's wish to Pope Pius XI. On March 19,

1930, the pope celebrated a "mass of penitence, reconciliation, and atonement for the many crimes that have been committed against Jesus, and for the liberation of the Russian people, so that their long persecution can come to an end." This was an acknowledgment of Lúcia's message, but it was not what the Madonna wanted.

By this time the predictions of the second secret of Fatima were beginning to come true, that "Russia will spread her mistakes throughout the world, starting wars and persecuting the Church. The good will be killed."

After the czar was assassinated in the Russian Revolution in 1917, the new leader, Vladimir Lenin, announced that "the way of terror is the only one that remains open for us, and we cannot avoid it." One of his first victims was the Orthodox Church. In November 1919 Patriarch Tikhon of Moscow sent out a desperate call for help to the world. "Bishops, priests, monks, and nuns have been executed under the vague accusation of being counterrevolutionary. They have been denied even the last rites and the relatives have been forbidden to give them a Christian burial."

Lenin's death in 1924 was followed by the rise of Joseph Stalin, "the man of steel," who founded the "Union of Militant Atheists," whose chief aim was to spread atheism and eradicate religion. In the following years it devastated hundreds of churches, destroyed old icons and relics, and persecuted the clergy with unimaginable brutality. On May 15, 1932, Stalin signed a "five-year plan against religion." By May 1, 1937, the "idea that there was a God" was to be eradicated completely from public life.

It is useless, at this point, to speculate about whether what happened in Europe could have been prevented. But the fact remains that the terrible events in Russia fulfilled the predictions of the Second Secret almost word for word.

CHAPTER NINE

A BLOODRED SKY

ON THE EVENING of January 25, 1938, the sky over Europe took on a bloodred color. People believed a gigantic fire had broken out, and sirens howled in all the major cities on the continent. In the whole Alpine region the horizon was so red, it looked as if dawn had already arrived. This phenomenon was seen all the way to the south, in Greece, Italy, Spain, and Portugal, past Sicily and Gibraltar, even in North Africa. Scientists said that it was a gigantic aurora borealis, northern lights of historical dimensions.

"A pale, beautiful, greenish-blue light enveloped the sky from northeast to northwest" was how the bulletin of the Astronomical Society of France described it. "Gradually, the sky turned a fiery red and an irregular red arch appeared. A cloudlike structure, tinged with purple, formed in the northeast and moved toward the northwest, as if propelled by an invisible wind. It vanished and then reappeared, while immense light rays, with colors that changed from bloodred to orange-red to yellow, rose up to the zenith of the sky, enveloping the stars. The spectacle was enchanting, but it created panic. In the streets one could hear, 'Paris is on fire!' In several villages firemen were mobilized."

Contemporary reports described the signs in the sky with dramatic expressions such as "the reflection of a monstrous inferno," and "heavenly fires of hell." It was said that "almost the entire sky stood in flames" "as if the heavens were burning," and "it looked as if the end of the world had come."

On this cold winter night, when the heavens seemed to be burning, a group of nuns stood on the terrace of the convent of Tui in Spain, observing the phenomenon with great concern. One of them was Lúcia.

She knew what it meant. In her memory the words of the Madonna were as fresh as if she had heard them only the day before. "When you see a night lit up by an unknown light, you'll know it's the sign given you by God, and that He is about to punish the world for its crimes, by war, hunger, and persecutions against the Church and the pope."

When she closed her eyes, she could see the pictures of hell that the Lady had shown her before revealing the second secret. It suddenly became clear to her that her mission regarding the first secret had failed, because pe^ple had not listened, and had not brought Russia back to God. Now even the Virgin herself could no longer hold back the inevitable repercussions.

The next day Lúcia sat down and wrote a long letter to her bishop, Canon Galamba, to the provincial mother superior, and to her father confessor, in which she declared, "God said that His justice will soon be used against the sinning nations." Only one thing, she was sure, could prevent the approaching catastrophe: the consecration of Russia. If that could happen, grace and forgiveness would come, "not only for the whole world, but especially for Europe."

But her plea went unheard. Although in June 1938 the Portuguese bishops decided at the Annual Congress at Fatima that they would beg the pope to perform the consecration of Russia to Mary, they received no reply from Rome.

"We are on the brink of the war that Our Dear Lady predicted," wrote Lúcia on February 6, 1939. "But Portugal will not be affected."

In March 1939 she had another vision, and received a new message: "Ask again and again for the celebration of communion in honor of Mary on the first Saturday of every month. The time is coming when my justice will punish nations for their crimes. Some of them will be wiped out."

Referring to this in a letter written on March 19, 1939, to her previous father confessor, Father Aparicio, she said, "Whether there will be world peace or a world war depends on what we do." In a sequel written June 20 she added, "Our Dear Lady promised to hold back the war if Her worship spreads to Russia. But I am afraid we can do nothing more, and that God will punish the world."

As a matter of fact the war that cost over fifty-five million people their lives had already begun. At about the same time as the blood-colored sky appeared in Europe, Adolf Hitler, in Berlin, was already preparing for the invasion of Austria. On March 12, 1938, German troops crossed the border for the first time since the end of World War I, and entered Austria, in order to "bring it back into the Reich."

Several months later, Nazi troops marched into the Sudetenland region of Czechoslovakia. World War II really began then, under the rule of Pius XI, exactly as prophesied at Fatima. On February 10, 1939, Pius XI died. He had been the great procrastinator, who warned Europe too late about the terrors he saw happening in the world, which only helped to establish the Soviet Union. He ignored the warnings of Fatima.

He was followed by a man who felt himself deeply connected with Fatima. Eugenio Pacelli, who became Pope Pius XII, had been consecrated as bishop on May 13, 1917, the very day and, as he said, "at the very hour when the white-robed Queen appeared above the hills of Fatima." When Sister Lúcia learned about the new pope, she was full of hope. It seemed that finally her words would be heard in Rome.

On August 18, 1940, she decided to write to the new pope directly. Lúcia wrote on October 24 to Pius XII, two days after Jesus had appeared to her once more threatening to "punish the nations for their crimes" by bringing about war, hunger, and religious persecution if the pope did not immediately make a special effort to convert Russia to the worship of Mary.

When Lúcia's first letter to the pope was censored by the bishop of Leiria, who felt it was too long, Lúcia sent off another version on December 2, 1940. It was another two years before the pope paid attention to her message.

War was spreading all over Europe, invading one country after another. On August 24, 1939, the foreign ministers of the Third Reich and the Soviet Union signed a pact of nonaggression in Moscow, dividing up the world between them.

On September 1, Hitler's troops swept into Poland. On September 2, Great Britain and France sent him an ultimatum demanding the end of all military action by September 3, 1939. When it was ignored, both nations declared war on Germany. With this the Second World War had officially begun.

Meanwhile, the twenty-fifth anniversary of Fatima was a triumph. The jubilee year was declared in February, and in April a huge Marian festival was held in Lisbon. The statue of Our Lady of Fatima was brought there in a solemn procession of over half a million people. An equal number of pilgrims were gathered at the Cova da Íria to attend festivities on May 13. Thousands of priests and all the bishops of Portugal had come to take part in the celebrations.

Cardinal Cerejeira, the patriarch of Lisbon, declared that "Fatima has not yet revealed all its secrets. But we feel justified in saying that what it has already done for Portugal is a sign that shows what it will do for the rest of the world. For what has happened here during the last twenty-five years, there is only one word: *Miracle!* We are firmly convinced that we have the most Holy Virgin to thank for the marvelous religious conversion that has taken place in Portugal."

A mass was celebrated at the end of the festival, on October 13, 1942, during which Portugal was consecrated anew to the worship of Mary by the cardinal of Lisbon and the bishops. For the first time the complete texts of the First and the Second Secrets of Fatima, as written down by Lúcia, were published. "We believe that the visions of Fatima marked the beginning of a new era," said the cardinal, as he concluded his speech.

During the jubilee year the Portuguese bishops once again sent a petition to Rome, begging the pope to consecrate Russia to the Mother of God. To their disappointment the Vatican remained silent until October 13, when it was suddenly and unexpectedly announced that the pope would send a message to the world on October 31, at the official end of the jubilee.

At 5:00 P.M. that day all the radio stations of Portugal broadcast the ringing of the bells of Saint Peter's, followed by a speech by Pope Pius XII. The entire nation was listening, and for those who did not own a radio, the Church put loudspeakers up in open places, where people could gather to listen. The pope said to the nation, in perfect Portuguese, "During the hours of darkness and despair heaven, which could foresee these dangers, intervened, and Portugal, the faithful, regained its role as a religious nation, thanks to the Holy Virgin, the Mother of that country, whose protection showed itself so clearly. At that time no one could imagine the horrors to come in 1936, when the Communist danger was so close.

"Today we are in the fourth year of that war. The more the conflict spreads, the more dangerous it becomes. Let us ask the Virgin for help once more, for She alone can help us."

Pope Pius XII fulfilled, at least in principle, the wish of the Madonna, by including a subtle reference to Russia, referring to "peoples separated by error and discord, where once there wasn't a single house that did not display Your holy icon, which today are hidden away until better days." However, it was by no means the consecration demanded by the Lady, a detail Lúcia pointed out to her friends shortly afterward.

Although the final goal, the conversion of Russia, remained unfulfilled, the ritual nevertheless seemed to have a positive effect. Toward the end of 1942 the Second World War took a sudden and unexpected turn, giving hope that perhaps the march of evil could be stopped.

And indeed, a miracle did happen. Three days after

the pope's broadcast, on November 3, 1942, following a bloody battle that had lasted ten days, the German troops suffered their first crushing defeat at the hands of the allies in Egypt. On November 8 British and American troops occupied North Africa. On the day when Pope Pius repeated the consecration, December 8, 1942, the battle of Stalingrad began, which ended the German march to the east and is considered the turning point of World War II. On February 2, 1943, after the loss of many lives, the German Sixth Army surrendered.

However, it is difficult to accept a connection between the Fatima consecration and these world events. In order for God to act, must we depend on a ritual being performed correctly by a single human being? This seems unfair and also absurd.

On the other hand, we have recently learned from experiments in parapsychology that thought, if powerful enough, can sometimes overcome the physical laws of nature. Perhaps the pope was important not so much because of his spiritual powers, but because he was the only person who could get the attention and support of all the Catholics in the world. This may have been an early experiment in channeling mental energy. The healing of the world had to come from those who made it sick in the first place: humanity itself.

"The good Lord has already shown me He is happy with the act performed by the pope and the bishops, although it was incomplete," wrote Lúcia on February 28, 1943, to the bishop of Gurza. "He promises in return to end the war soon. The conversion of Russia is not going to come about at this time." And that is exactly how things happened.

By now the Vatican was prepared to listen to her. When she begged the pope "to set aside a feast day to honor Mary, which will be celebrated in the whole world as one of the major feasts of the church," Pius XII granted her request. On May 4, 1944, the Holy Father announced the creation of a new feast day in honor of the Immaculate Heart of Mary, to be celebrated every year on August 22.

A year later the war had come to an end, but the world had not yet found peace. At the Yalta conference on February 4 through 11, 1945, the future division of Europe was settled. The whole of Eastern Europe was assigned to the Soviet Union. Once-free nations were wiped out or made puppets of the USSR. As the Lady had predicted, "Russia will spread its mistakes throughout the world, starting wars and persecuting the Church. The good will be killed. The pope will suffer, nations will be destroyed."

On May 13, 1946, the statue of the Madonna at Fatima was crowned in a great ceremony. The Portuguese, whose country had been protected from the devastation of war, expressed their thanks to the Lady who had saved them. The golden crown, embedded with precious gems, had been made by melting down jewelry donated by the women of Portugal. At noon on that day the image was brought from the chapel in a solemn

procession to the court of the basilica. Shortly afterward
the pope broadcast a special message of thanks over the
radio to the Portuguese nation.

On November 26 the newly crowned Queen of
Fatima went on a triumphal tour through Portugal. During this procession what became known as the "miracle
of the doves" occurred for the first time. Six white doves
were released as a sign of peace. Five of these doves flew
to the image and sat around its feet. Even when people
tried to drive them away, they returned to the same spot
and remained there, despite the bad weather, until the
ceremony was over on December 9, 1946. After that,
they flew away and were never seen again.

When the statue was taken to its next station, doves
were released again. This time one dove flew to the image and stayed at its feet for a whole week. Later, on
December 21, a boy released four doves, and three of
them went back and took their positions at the feet of the
statue. This miracle was to repeat itself on many more
occasions when, during 1947, the statue of the Madonna
was brought to other European countries and after that to
the United States and Canada. Pope Pius XII described it
as a "pilgrimage of miracles."

A week after the ceremony crowning the statue of the
Lady of Fatima, Lúcia returned for the first time in
twenty-five years to the Cova da Íria. When she discovered there was a newly built Carmelite convent near the
site of the visions, she remembered her old wish and
again wanted to enter the Carmelite order. She wrote to

the pope, asking for his permission, and her request was granted. On May 13, 1948, Lúcia entered the order of the Carmelite nuns as Sister Maria Lúcia of the Immaculate Heart. The Carmelite convent of Coimbra in North Portugal became her new home. With that she withdrew from the world.

Her withdrawal into the strict and almost total seclusion of the Carmelite order suited the opponents of Fatima only too well. During the two years before she went there, Lúcia had repeatedly written to church officials, emphasizing the need to specifically consecrate Russia to the worship of Mary.

But there were people in the Vatican who were not at all in favor of this step. Their aim was to first establish diplomatic connections with Moscow. The Soviets might interpret such a papal proclamation as a deliberate act of intervention in their internal affairs. They felt that it would be irresponsible for the pope to perform a naive and sentimental act that could jeopardize all their hopes for obtaining relief for the Christians in Russia. An official statement was made that "no pope has ever consecrated any country in which non-Christians or Protestants are in the majority."

"Rome's attitude toward Fatima is reported to have changed considerably," said a press report. "The short period of popularity and enthusiasm has given way to one of coolness, indifference, and disillusion." Someone even repeated that the pope had said he did not want to hear anything more about Fatima.

"People have invented these things to serve their own purposes," stated Pope Pius XII indignantly, when confronted with the rumors about papal indifference toward Fatima. "Tell them that the thoughts of the pope are completely in agreement with the message of Fatima. They should continue to worship Our Dear Lady of the Rosary of Fatima with reverence and enthusiasm."

During a papal audience in 1951 someone called out, "Long live the pope of Fatima!" Pius XII answered with a smile, "That's me!"

Nevertheless the "pope of Fatima" did not succeed in overcoming the opposition in the Vatican to performing the act desired by the Madonna. Pius XII was a man of compromise, who tried to please everyone and avoided confrontation. His inability to stand firm and fight for his convictions was his undoing in the early years of his papacy, in his confrontation with Hitler and later with the Nazis in Rome. Although it has been historically proven that he helped thousands of Jews to escape, the fact is that he never spoke out openly against Hitler's anti-Semitism, and this made him a target of criticism. He showed the same "adaptability" in his dealings with Fatima, although heaven did everything it could to remind him of his obligation.

On October 29, 1950, the wandering Madonna of Fatima arrived in Rome, after having traveled through Asia. The next day the pope had a vision in the garden of the Vatican, where the "dance of the sun" of Fatima repeated itself.

"It was about four o'clock in the afternoon," the pope himself wrote later. "I was taking my daily walk in the Vatican gardens, reading and studying various official papers. I went up the Esplanade of Our Lady of Lourdes, to the top of the hill, in the passage on the right near the walls.

"At a certain moment, lifting my eyes from the papers in my hand, I was struck by a phenomenon that I had never seen before. The sun, which was fairly high, looked like a pale, yellow, opaque globe, completely surrounded by a luminous halo, which, nevertheless, did not prevent me from staring at the sun without the slightest discomfort. A small cloud was in front of it. The globe began moving outward, slowly rotating, going from left to right, then reversing direction. The same thing repeated on the following day, then on November 1, and once more on November 8. Since then there has been nothing more." When the pope asked the Vatican observatory if anything unusual had been reported during those periods, the reply was negative.

"Let the Holy Father know that I am still waiting for the consecration of Russia," declared the Madonna to Sister Lúcia during a new vision in May 1952. "Without this Russia cannot be converted and the world cannot find peace."

When Lúcia wrote a personal letter to the pope, telling him this, he decided on a final compromise. On July 7, 1952, he composed a pastoral letter, addressed to the people of Russia, in which he condemned the errors of godless Communism and called for the veneration of the Virgin Mary. This was well meant, but for Lúcia, it wasn't enough.

On September 8, 1953, Pius XII declared 1954 to be a Marian year. But he made no reference to the Lady of Fatima. Eventually the pope ordered that Sister Lúcia was only allowed to meet with those people whom she was already in contact with, and anyone else who wanted to meet her would have to get permission from the Vatican. The Carmelite convent of Lúcia's order said, "Sister Lúcia has said everything about Fatima that she wanted, and had, to say." But the last words about Fatima had not yet been spoken. The Third Secret that the Madonna had revealed to the three children would become the most zealously guarded secret of the Vatican.

CHAPTER TEN

THE THIRD SECRET

DURING THE SUMMER of 1941 Sister Lúcia mentioned for the first time, in the third volume of her memoirs, that the secret which the Mother of God had given to her on July 13, 1917, was in three parts and that she "would now reveal the first two parts." At that time she wrote down the first two prophecies, which related to the end of World War I, the rise of Russia, and the breaking out of World War II. She believed, however, that the time for publishing the Third Secret had not yet come, and wrote down only the first words of it, "In Portugal the doctrine of faith will always be preserved."

In the summer of 1943 Sister Lúcia caught bronchitis, which developed into a dangerous pleurisy. Luckily, she soon recovered. When Bishop da Silva and Canon Galamba visited her at her cloister afterward, they had a long talk with her. They were worried that she might fall seriously ill again and die, carrying her secret with her into the grave.

"Why don't you reveal the third part of the secret?" asked the canon. "Can't you tell us now?"

Lúcia replied, turning to the bishop, "If Your Grace wishes it, I can tell you."

"I don't want to have anything to do with it," answered the bishop hastily. "I don't wish to intervene in the matter in any way."

"What a pity!" said the canon with a sigh. "At least she should write it down and leave it with you in a sealed envelope." But nothing was done at that time.

Then, in September 1943, Sister Lúcia was once again ill, this time due to a severe infection following a vaccination. She had to be taken to the hospital and was operated on there. When she returned to the cloister three weeks later, everyone begged her to finally put the prophecy down in writing. She waited for divine instructions, and it wasn't until January 1944 that she told the bishop of Leiria, "I have written down what you wanted me to. God wanted to test me for a while, but finally this was indeed His will. It is in a sealed envelope in my diary."

She revealed later that she had been encouraged to write down the secret by a vision of Mary she saw on January 2. Until then, despite repeated attempts to recall the exact words of the prophecy, she had been unable to do so. But after the appearance of the Madonna the words flowed out of her pen. She immediately wrote it down in twenty-five lines, which was as long as the first two secrets put together, but still fitted easily onto a single page of paper.

Lúcia did not trust this valuable document to the mail, but waited for a suitable opportunity to give it to Bishop da Silva. Finally, on July 17, 1944, she handed over her fourth diary. She had inserted the envelope containing the Third Secret between two of its pages. In an accompanying letter Lúcia suggested that the secret should be kept at Leiria until the death of da Silva, but after that it should be given to the cardinal of Lisbon.

Bishop da Silva, on the other hand, wanted to send it to Rome. But the Vatican instructed him to keep the envelope at Leiria for the present. Da Silva put the still unopened envelope into a larger one, sealed it with wax, and wrote on it, "This envelope with its contents shall be handed over after my death to His Eminence Don Manuel, cardinal of Lisbon."

Later on he declared, "I didn't want to read it; Fatima is entirely God's work and I did not want to interfere in it. I could have opened the letter if I had wanted to, but I chose not to. It is not my business to intervene in this matter. The secrets of heaven are not meant for me and I will not take on the responsibilities they involve." Canon Galamba confirmed that "the secret could have been revealed at once, if the bishop had wanted it. But Lúcia did not say that it should be opened immediately."

Sister Lúcia tried repeatedly to get an audience with

Pope Pius XII, to personally tell him about the contents of the Third Secret. After these attempts failed, Canon Galamba said, "When the bishop refused to open the envelope, Lúcia made him promise that the contents would be published after her death, or in the year 1960, whichever occurred first."

During the following years Lúcia frequently talked about this compromise. At times she seemed to contradict herself. On February 13, 1946, during a conversation with a priest, she declared, "I have given the contents of the third revelation in a letter to the bishop of Leiria. But it cannot be published before 1960." On August 12, 1946, in another conversation, she said, "The bishop can open the secret. He doesn't have to wait till 1960." Again, on May 17, 1955, she said, "The message should not be opened until 1960, because it will be much clearer then."

But before then Rome intervened. Early in 1957 the Holy Office asked the bishop of Leiria for photocopies of everything that had been written by Sister Lúcia. The bishop asked whether that included the secret that was still in the sealed envelope. The answer was "Yes, of course it includes the secret, especially the secret!"

By that time the bishop was eighty-five years old and very weak, pained by rheumatism, and almost blind. His secretary said to him, "Your Grace, here is the secret. You can read it. Lúcia said you could open it. Please open it! We can make a photocopy of it. It is our last chance." But he refused. "No, it doesn't interest me," he said. "It's a secret and I don't want to read it."

The secretary then took the envelope to Bishop Venancio. He held it up to the light and tried to read what he could. Within the larger envelope he could see a smaller one, most likely the one from Sister Lúcia, and inside that envelope was a folded sheet of ordinary letter paper, with some lines of writing on it.

During March 1957 Bishop Venancio visited the Vatican diplomatic office in Lisbon to hand over the documents, which included the envelope, still sealed with wax. He admitted how reluctant he was to part with it. "It will be much safer in Rome than with you," he was told. The pope wanted to have the secret under his control in order to prevent it from falling into the wrong hands, even by mistake.

The envelope was kept in the most secure part of the Vatican, the private quarters of Pope Pius XII. When the French journalist Robert Serrou of *Paris Match* was given permission to photograph the pope's private apartment on May 14, 1957, he noticed a small wooden safe standing on a table, bearing the words "Secret of the Holy Office."

"What's in it?" he asked the pope's housekeeper.

"The Third Secret of Fatima" was her reply. Naturally, the photograph of the safe was the main item in Serrou's article. Did Pius XII ever read the document? Probably not. One can assume that he, too, was waiting for 1960, the magical date set for the opening of the seal.

But it was not to be. He died on October 9, 1958, a year after the death of da Silva, the bishop of Leiria. When the envelope was brought to his successor, Pope John XXIII, at Castelgondolfo, the seal on the envelope was still intact.

But fourteen months after the secret was brought to Rome, a leak occurred. On December 26, 1957, Sister Lúcia was visited by a Mexican priest, Father Fuentes. They spoke to each other for hours. The situation of the world came up, and Lúcia hinted at the contents of the third revelation.

On May 22, 1958, after his return to Mexico, Father Fuentes gave a lecture at a missionary to a group of nuns. During his speech he talked about the important parts of his conversation with Sister Lúcia. Soon after that he published the text of his speech.

"When I met her at her convent," he said, "she was very pale and exhausted, and very sad. The first thing she said to me was 'Father, the Most Holy Virgin is filled with sorrow, for no one pays any attention to her message.' "

One of the things he reported she said was "Tell them, Father, that the Most Holy Virgin told my cousins, Francisco and Jacinta, and me, that many nations will vanish from the face of the earth. She said that Russia would be the instrument of punishment, if we do not convert that poor nation before it happens."

"What saddens her most," he said, "is the fall of the souls of the priests and members of religious orders. The devil knows that the souls of the clergy, who fall from their glorious calling, drag countless souls with them into hell."

Lúcia also told him that "the Most Holy Virgin did not tell me that we are living through the last days of the world, but I understood that we are."

The publication of Father Fuentes's speech set off a scandal. He was accused of having taken advantage of his visit to Sister Lúcia for the sake of making sensational statements. Owing to his indiscretion Father Fuentes was relieved of his office by the Vatican.

When, early in 1959, a high official in the Vatican suggested to Pope John XXIII that Sister Lúcia be permitted to speak to the world over the radio, he turned him down. "It seemed as if he personally preferred her to be silent," his private secretary wrote later. Rome was preparing for the Second Vatican Council, and the air was filled with a sense of hope and a new beginning. No one wanted to listen to "prophets of doom," as John XXIII called them. Was he hinting that the Third Secret had a depressing message for the world?

Finally, the person who was in charge of keeping the envelope safe asked him, "Holy Father, don't you want to see it?"

He answered, "I'll let you know when you should bring it to me." Some time elapsed. When he went to Castelgondolfo in August for the summer holidays, he was surrounded by peace and quiet, so perhaps he felt the time had come. Thus Pope John decided to do what his predecessor, out of respect for a falsely interpreted date, had not had the courage to do: he opened the envelope containing the message of Fatima.

On August 17, 1959, John XXIII read the text of the Third Secret slowly, with trembling hands. The text was difficult and since he did not speak Portuguese, he had to get help from an interpreter more than once. His confessor was there as well, to give him support and encouragement. When he realized what it was all about, his face turned white as chalk.

The three men sat and discussed the contents of Lúcia's writing until late at night, then the pontiff made his decision. "I cannot publish this and will not publish it. I'll leave it for others to do so. It is certain that it does not deal with my reign." He put Lúcia's letter back in its envelope, together with a personal note in which he wrote down the reasons for his decision. Back in Rome he called his closest advisors together and told them about the contents of the secret as well as his decision not to make them public. He made them all swear to keep the secret.

The French author Jacques Vallée quotes a Vatican insider regarding this secret meeting. "The meeting was strictly confidential and took place in the pope's study. A secretary saw the cardinals when they came out of the room, and said their expressions were filled with horror. The secretary stood up and approached one of them, whom he knew well. But he was gently but firmly pushed aside by the pope, who went past as if he had seen a ghost."

At the "Fatima 2000" Conference in November 1995 the former secretary of Cardinal Bea, Dr. Malachi Martin, recalled the reaction of the cardinal after he left the secret meeting. He said that the cardinal was obviously shaken, but also annoyed that the pope would not publish the Third Secret. Dr. Martin was later told the contents of the Third Secret by Pope John.

The closer the year 1960 approached, the more feverishly Catholics looked forward to the revelation of the "Third Secret." There was hardly a newspaper around that did not speculate about the contents of the revelation and the date on which the Holy Father would publish it. May 13, 1960, the forty-third anniversary of the first apparition, was the favorite guess. The feelings of the public veered between hopeful expectation and dread that they were going to hear negative prophecies. Suddenly an announcement came from the Rome office of the Portuguese news agency on February 8, destroying all hopes of an early publication.

It said, "The Secret of Fatima is not to be published at all, according to sources in the Vatican. Reliable circles in the Vatican have informed the United Press International that the letter, in which Sister Lúcia wrote down the message given to the three little shepherds at the Cova da Íria, has never been opened.

"As Sister Lúcia hinted," the announcement continued, "the letter can be opened only in 1960. Because of the pressure on the Vatican by those who want the letter to be published, and the fears of others that it may contain alarming prophecies, the Vatican has decided not to open Sister Lúcia's letter, but to keep it sealed. It is likely that the secret of Fatima will remain sealed forever."

This clearly went against the wishes of the Lady herself. The announcement was also filled with mistakes. For one, Sister Lúcia never said that the letter could be opened "only" in 1960. The year 1960 was the latest possible date for opening it. Also, the seal of the letter had already been broken six months before, by Pope John XXIII.

Referring to the announcement, the cardinal of Lisbon declared on February 24, 1960, "I was not consulted in this matter. What I know about the intention not to publish is what I read in the papers."

Only years later did John XXIII mention the secret to him, "in vague words, very generally. I realized it was a very serious matter. If it had been joyous, I would have been told about it. Since nothing specific was said, it means that it is very sad."

John XXIII kept the Fatima message on his desk during the rest of his period in office, until his death on June 3, 1963. Can we deduce from this behavior that he attached no importance to the third message? "Quite the contrary," declared Father José Geraldes Freire, an authority regarding Fatima. "I have evidence that John XXIII gave the message great importance, and that certain major decisions, which many found inexplicable, were influenced by it."

CHAPTER ELEVEN
THE DIPLOMATIC VERSION

ON OCTOBER 15, 1963, a way out of the dilemma was found. The German magazine *European News,* citing an inside source at the Vatican, published a "diplomatic version" of the third secret of Fatima, which had allegedly been sent by the Vatican to the governments of Washington, London, and Moscow during the height of the Cuban Missile Crisis a year earlier.

According to the magazine the agreement signed by the foreign ministers of the United Kingdom and Russia, and the U.S. secretary of state, to stop atomic bomb tests, was "due to intervention by the Vatican. It was, in fact, the first time in modern history that these governments took religious information into consideration. Pope Paul permitted not only Kennedy (who was a Catholic), but also Khrushchev, to look at portions of the third message of Fatima, which the Mother of God revealed to the young Portuguese girl Lúcia on October 13, 1917. This message is of such importance that even the delegates from Moscow were deeply impressed by it."

In October 1962 the world stood on the edge of destruction. The crisis was set off when President Kennedy announced that the U.S. had discovered and photographed the setting up of Soviet medium-range missiles on the island of Cuba. Kennedy reacted by sending U.S. warships to Cuba. The Soviet Union and Cuba countered by mobilizing their armed forces. The whole world feared the immediate outbreak of a third world war, which, they were certain, would end in an all-out nuclear conflagration.

But first the diplomats had a chance to meet. The UN secretary general U Thant told the heads of state in Washington, Havana, and Moscow that he would help mediate the discussion, at the request of forty-five other UN member nations. Pope John XXIII appealed to the world on October 25, desperately pleading for peace. The tension relaxed when Nikita Khrushchev accepted U Thant's offer and ordered Soviet vessels heading for Cuba to change course. But the U.S. still insisted on the dismantling of the missiles on Cuba. Finally on October 28 Khrushchev agreed to this as well, after extracting a guarantee from the U.S. that they would not invade Cuba.

Finally, on August 5, 1963, the treaty to stop atomic bomb tests was signed in Moscow. Did the Fatima message really play a role in this drama? Did John XXIII reveal some of its contents to the leaders of the major powers during the Cuban crisis? And if he did, did this religious message actually have an influence on them? We do not know.

Louis Emrich, editor of *European News,* wrote, "I have tried everything possible to get the original text of the Fatima message, but all my efforts have been in vain. The Vatican has taken all precautions to make sure that the document remains a papal secret. Nevertheless I am in a position today to reveal an extract from the text of the Third Secret in the form in which it was made available to diplomatic circles in Washington, London, and Moscow. Although the document does not contain the original text of the message of Fatima as revealed to Lúcia by the Mother of God on October 13, 1917, the essential points of the original are present in it.

"It was on the thirteenth of October 1917. On this day the Holy Virgin appeared for the last time before the little visionaries Jacinta, Francisco, and Lúcia, at the end of a series of appearances, totaling six in all. After the 'dance of the sun' the Mother of God revealed a secret message especially to Lúcia, in which she said, 'Do not be afraid, my little one, for I am the Mother of God speaking to you, and I ask you to give this message to the whole world. When you do this, you will meet with strong opposition, so listen carefully and note what I say to you. Men must become better. They must beg for forgiveness for all the sins they have committed and are committing.

" 'A severe punishment will come to the whole of mankind, not today, not tomorrow, but in the second half of the twentieth century. . . . Satan reigns even in the highest places and directs the course of events. He will even know how to find his way to the highest positions in the Church. He will succeed in sowing confusion in the minds of the great scientists, who will invent weapons with which half of humanity can be destroyed within a few minutes. He will make the mighty follow him and lead them to manufacture such weapons in huge quantities. . . . If those at the top, in the world and in the Church, do not oppose these ways, it is I who shall do so, and I shall ask God my Father to visit His justice on mankind. And see, God will punish men still more severely and heavily than He did by means of the Flood, and the great and powerful will perish just as much as the small and the weak. . . .

" 'The great war will break out in the second half of the twentieth century. Fire and smoke will fall from the sky, the waters of the oceans will turn into steam and sizzle up to the heavens, everything that stands will tumble down. Millions and millions of people will lose their lives and those that survive will envy the dead. Misery, suffering, and destruction will be everywhere, in all the lands. . . . Go, my child, and proclaim this.' "

Closing this report, the editor stated, "I must once more add that this is not the text of the original message, but only an extract from the Third Message of Fatima, as it is being circulated at present in diplomatic circles. I was assured that the authentic wording of the message was more harsh and overpowering than in the version given above."

However, this "diplomatic version" cannot be genuine for several reasons. For one thing, there was no revelation given to Lúcia after the Dance of the Sun. All three of the secrets of Fatima were given to the children by the Holy Virgin before the sun miracle of October 13, 1917. The first two were published at once and were never a secret.

Also, the "diplomatic version" is described as being only an extract, but it is far too long. The original fitted onto a small sheet of paper, consisting of about twenty-five lines, and was not much longer than the first and second parts of the message put together, which made up twenty-three handwritten lines. The version quoted in the news magazine is at least three times that long.

And Lúcia herself said that the authentic version must begin with the words "In Portugal the doctrine of faith will always be preserved," although this introduction may have been left out of the "extract."

Had Emrich invented this just to get a story, or had he heard genuine rumors from the Vatican? This question was investigated by the well-known German parapsychologist Hans Bender in 1981, seven years after Emrich's death. He questioned Emrich's widow about the circumstances under which her husband had published the "diplomatic version." Bender summarized her reply, "Emrich worked on the Fatima story for quite some time before the publication on October 15, 1963, and already had some information about the probable contents of the document guarded by the Vatican as a state secret. Then a priest from the Vatican visited him, who clearly emphasized that he had not been sent officially, but that he had come for his own reasons."

The meeting between Emrich and the priest lasted the whole afternoon. After that Emrich said that he could now understand why they were keeping it secret. What was coming was terrible. Now he felt he must and could write about it, for he had received information that agreed with the rumors he had heard before. Based on his notes he put together the "diplomatic version" of the message of Fatima.

When asked about the motives of the priest, Mrs. Emrich replied, "He was a reader of *European News* and had kept issues in which my husband had predicted the Second World War. He had the feeling that it was time to open the eyes of people everywhere, and tell them what was ahead. He felt an urgent need to see my husband and talk to him about it."

Mrs. Emrich told Professor Bender that the version printed in the magazine was based on notes made during the conversation with a mysterious priest.

The main question here is, was the visit by the priest official or unofficial? Even though the visit was secretive, it could have been part of a plan of deliberate disinformation. *Disinformation* is a term in spy jargon that can be best explained by quoting Winston Churchill, who said, "One hides a truth most effectively between two lies." It is interesting to note that publication in a minor magazine like *European News* would never get the kind of publicity that a serious newspaper would bring. Those who wanted to believe in it could do so. But if the reaction was too negative, it could easily be officially denied. Interestingly enough, the Emrich version was never either confirmed or denied by the Church.

Could the Vatican have used the Third Secret to change the course of history? Did they decide to keep the actual words secret so that they could "create" an appropriate message during times of international emergency? In any case the followers of Fatima, who had demanded the release of the secret since 1960, were now satisfied, at least for the time being, despite the fact that they had heard something that confirmed their worst fears. Most important of all, the Vatican could now take credit for having saved the world during the greatest threat to peace since the end of World War II, by means of the kind of diplomacy that reinforced the Church's teachings.

Vatican radio announced on May 13, 1977, that neither Pope John XXIII nor Pope Paul VI considered it right to reveal the contents of the third part of the Secret of Fatima to the world at large. It is possible that the whole scheme was thought up by the newly elected Pope Paul VI, who had most certainly read the Fatima message, as well as the note written by his predecessor. Monsignor Capovilla affirmed that "after his election Paul VI asked for all information regarding this document. I don't remember whether it was in July 1963 or a few months later, but we can believe that he read the message."

On another occasion Capovilla added, "Paul VI asked me, 'What was the opinion of Pope John XXIII?' Perhaps he wanted to know more, but I could only say what I knew, which was that his decision was 'I will leave it to my successors.' And Paul VI said, 'I shall do that too.' "

Officially, the Vatican declared silence regarding the matter, a silence that lasted until the fiftieth anniversary of the events at Fatima. During the start of preparations for the jubilee celebrations on February 11, 1967, Cardinal Ottaviani gave a speech at the Papal Marian Academy, in which he laid down the future course of action regarding the "Third Secret" as ordained by the pope. It said, "The third secret will not be released, for it is addressed to the pope and only to him." Of course, we know this isn't true.

He also said, "The devoted must be content with the appeal to prayer and penance, which was given to them at Lourdes. There is no sense in discussing the contents of the Third Secret, for no part of it has been revealed." We know that this also is not true, because Lúcia revealed the first few words.

He went on to say, "One does not have to be afraid of the contents of the message. Fatima is not a frightening message, but a message of hope." If the "diplomatic version" published in *European News* was real, then this statement would not be true either.

The three little seers in the year 1917: Lúcia, Francisco, and Jacinta.

The children on July 13, 1917, after their "vision of hell" and the revelation of the three secrets.

October 13, 1917: The children are brought to the apparition site, Jacinta in the arms of a man.

October 13, 1917: Pilgrims in the Cova da Íria, in the heavy rain.

The rain has stopped, the apparition begins, and the believers kneel down.

Thousands observe the Miracle of the Sun.

The little chapel at the apparition site, in front of the oak over which the Madonna appeared, before its destruction of March 6, 1922.

RIGHT. Pope John Paul II and Sister Lúcia on May 13, 1982.

BELOW. The sanctuary of Fatima today, with the huge basilica in the center.

The undecayed body of Jacinta, exhumed on September 12, 1935.

Pope John Paul II during the consecration of Russia on March 25, 1984.

The little seers of Heroldsbach.

The four seer children of Garabandal in July, 1961.

LEFT. From August 29 to September 1, 1953, an image of the Madonna in Sicily cried real tears.

BELOW. The Madonna of Verona, Italy, that has cried blood 120 times, shown on March 14, 1995.

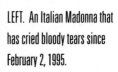

LEFT. An Italian Madonna that has cried bloody tears since February 2, 1995.

The Miracle of the Sun in Belpasso, Sicily, on February 1, 1988. Two suns appeared, one formed from a luminous disk.

A cross of clouds appeared in 1988 in Belpasso, Sicily.

Later on in his declaration Cardinal Ottaviani referred to Jacinto and Francisco as Lúcia's "brother and sister." Finally, he said, "Although I am bound to secrecy, I had the good fortune to read the message, so I can say that the rumors going around are based on superstitious fantasy." But if he had read it, he would know that the three children were cousins and not siblings.

Vatican observers were surprised when the pope himself traveled to Fatima on May 13, 1967, the fiftieth anniversary of the first apparition. It was only his fourth journey abroad. He landed at the military airport of Monte Real, where he was received by the president of Portugal. Thousands of people lined the thirty-mile-long road leading from the airport to Fatima, to see Paul VI driving past in an old, white, open Rolls-Royce embellished with the papal coat of arms.

The weather was cool, almost like winter, with showers and gusty winds. Standing up in the car, dressed in a white cassock, and protected from the weather by a dark red raincoat, the pope acknowledged the cheers of the people. Three million Portuguese had come to the village in the Serra de Aire to visit the Cova da Íria, the place consecrated by the Virgin herself.

Eventually the convoy of cars reached the place of pilgrimage, the guides managing somehow to clear a way through the crowds. There, on a platform at the foot of the basilica, the pontiff was to say mass and pray in seven languages to the Virgin of Fatima for the sake of a world threatened by famine and war.

Collected around him were the bishops of Portugal, hundreds of priests, representatives of the royal houses of Spain and Italy, members of the diplomatic corps—and one solitary nun, who felt overwhelmed by this massive demonstration of faith, which was in sharp contrast to the solitude of her cloister. This was Sister Lúcia, who had been permitted to leave the Carmelite nunnery to attend this function and visit her native village for only the second time since 1921.

The pope celebrated mass in Portuguese. He spoke about what everyone was convinced was the core of the Third Secret of Fatima. He knew that every word he uttered would be examined carefully to see if it held a hidden reference to the message. And those who looked for this were not disappointed. The pope's speech gave the impression that he had at least been inspired by the Third Secret of Fatima.

Part of his talk went as follows: "The present situation of mankind seems to be particularly serious: we possess a large number of horrifying weapons, but we are morally much less advanced than we are in science and technology. . . . We therefore say, 'The world is in danger!' That is why we have come, to kneel at the feet of the Queen of Peace, to ask Her for a gift that only God can give: peace."

During the same year, 1967, Cardinal Luciani, the patriarch of Venice, went to Coimbra to celebrate mass at the chapel of the cloister of the Carmelites, and had a private talk with Sister Lúcia for two hours. According to one of the people who accompanied him "the cardinal came out of the room, pale, as if he had seen a ghost, and this impression was shared by all of us in the group."

Luciani, who was usually jovial and unperturbed, seemed to be crushed by a heavy burden. Shortly after that, while visiting his family, he became deeply depressed. His sister-in-law recalled asking him if anything had gone wrong. "I can't help thinking over what Sister Lúcia told me at Coimbra," he replied. "The secret—it is terrible!"

CHAPTER TWELVE

DECODING THE SECRET

A YEAR LATER Cardinal Luciani was elected pope. We would expect that one of his first actions as Pope John Paul I would have been to read Sister Lúcia's handwritten text of the third part of the secret. It is not known whether he intended to publish it. After only thirty-three days in the Vatican "the smiling pope" broke down under the burden of his office and died, officially as the result of a heart attack.

What happened after his premature and mysterious death seemed to fulfill some sort of destiny regarding the Church. On Friday, October 13, 1978, on the sixty-first anniversary of the "dance of the sun," the cardinals arrived in Rome to elect the next pope.

It took only three days for them to elect Karol Cardinal Wojtyla, the archbishop of Kraków, who chose the name John Paul II to express his intention to follow in the footsteps of his predecessor. He declared that he wanted to become a Marian pope and announced that he would use the M of "Mary" on his seal.

But the day before he was elected, on October 15, 1978, Rome woke up to a bombshell. While the cardinals were locked in seclusion from the world, the Roman paper *L'Osservatore della Domenica* published an article on the Third Secret of Fatima. This was remarkable for two reasons. First of all, the paper is the Sunday edition of the Vatican's only official newspaper, *L'Osservatore Romano*. Second, the author of the article, "Prophecy and Reality," was a person of high standing within the Vatican, Monsignor Corrado Balducci, a former diplomat for the Vatican. "True or not, I wish to report it," he wrote, and quoted a few passages from the "diplomatic version," then went on to say, "The rumors had been that [the Third Secret] would be made public in 1960; then it was thought it would be during the Holy Year of 1975. If it had been good news, there would have been no reason not to divulge it. Unfortunately it seems to contain painful and very tragic predictions."

Balducci called the Emrich version "a text of acceptable authenticity, which causes us to reflect. . . . At this point, however, I want to examine the realities of the present, I want to shatter the dream in which we seem to be living, as if we were ignorant about what is ahead of us.

"Let us ask ourselves the first question: Is there a possibility of a world war breaking out? And then the second question: Who is so naive as to believe that a future war will not be fought with nuclear weapons? That would lead to an unprecedented apocalypse, to the destruction of mankind. One is reminded of Einstein's answer to a question about how a third world war would end: 'I don't know. One thing, however, is certain—should any other war occur after that, it will be fought with bows and arrows.' "

While Balducci's statement was ominous, it was as frustrating as all the other official revelations, because it basically told us no details at all. At that time, what was known about the contents of the Third Secret? First, it must have some relation, with regard to time sequence, to the other two parts of the revelation, which refer to the end of World War I, and to the outbreak of "another, even worse war," announced by "an unknown light" in the sky. We know that "Russia will spread her mistakes . . . nations will be destroyed." In the end, if the pope consecrates Russia to the Holy Virgin, that nation will be converted and the world will be blessed with a period of peace.

We knew that the secret must be connected with events that "could be understood better after 1960," as Lúcia said. During the early sixties two events occurred that could be relevant: the threat of an atomic war (the Cuba crisis) and the Second Vatican Council, with its consequences regarding the beliefs of Catholics everywhere.

There must have been a reason why five popes, Pius XII, John XXIII, Paul VI, and John Paul I and II, kept it under lock and key. We knew it must contain bad news, especially for the Church. To quote the cardinal of Lisbon, "If it had been joyous, I would have been told about it."

Father Joaquín Maria Alonso was firmly convinced that the third part of the secret spoke about a crisis in the Roman Catholic Church. He is acknowledged to be a leading expert in matters concerning Fatima. He felt that the text must make concrete predictions about a crisis in the Church and negligence on the part of its leaders. This would certainly be something the Church would want kept secret. When we think of the scandals of the past, of Catholic clergy helping Nazis to escape from Germany, and of the present, when pedophile priests are being convicted in courts of law, we can understand why.

Father Alonso's opinion was confirmed by Father Schweigl, who interviewed Sister Lúcia on September 2, 1952, at her convent at Coimbra, on instructions from Pope Pius XII. On his return to Rome, Schweigl declared, "I cannot reveal what I learned at Fatima about the Third Secret, but I can say that it has two parts, and one refers to the pope. The other—although I am not allowed to say anything—must be the continuation of the words: 'In Portugal the doctrine of faith will always be preserved.' " This implied that the opposite would happen—that faith would be lost—in the rest of the world.

Alberto Cosme do Amaral, bishop of Leiria and Fatima, stated in a speech on September 10, 1984, "The Secret of Fatima refers neither to atomic bombs, nor to nuclear warheads or Pershing rockets or SS-20s. Its contents deal only with our faith. To identify the Secret with prophecies about disaster or a nuclear holocaust twists the meaning of the message. The loss of faith on one continent is worse than the destruction of a nation; and it is true that the faith is continually disappearing in Europe."

Dr. Malachi Martin, former secretary of Cardinal Bea, was told about the contents during a secret meeting with Pope John XXIII. He said at the "Fatima 2000" conference in November 1995, "The contents of the Third Secret deal with a crisis of the kind which has never occurred in modern Catholicism, and the inability of the hierarchy to tackle this adequately." According to Dr. Martin, Cardinal Bea was very annoyed that the pope wanted to hide this.

Did the Fatima secret, therefore, deal primarily with a crisis in the Church and the loss of faith in Europe? If that were true, it would explain why its contents would be better understood after 1960. And indeed, the sixties were the beginning of widespread cynicism with regard to traditional religious beliefs, a feeling that has continued to gain ground in the western world.

On January 25, 1959, Pope John XXIII announced his intention to convene an ecumenical council, before he had read the Third Secret. Vatican II was opened on October 11, 1962, with a speech in which the Holy Father raised his voice "against the prophets of doom, who always announce the coming of ominous events, as if the end of the world stood before us." He had read Lúcia's secret by then, so was he referring to its contents when he talked about "prophets of doom"?

Vatican II, which was heralded at the time as a breakthrough for the Church, became the starting point for the biggest crisis the Catholic Church had faced in two thousand years. Millions of Catholics rejected the new style of mass and the new doctrines it implied. When told they no longer needed to go to confession, many stopped attending church altogether.

"The last ten years were markedly unfavorable for the Church," admitted Cardinal Ratzinger in 1984, during an interview with an Italian journalist. Ratzinger is a conservative member of the Vatican, whose name has been brought up many times as a possible candidate for the papacy.

Ratzinger spoke of the Church becoming demystified and too secular. This resulted in believers gradually losing all feeling for the Church as a "mysterious, superhuman reality," which was why he felt that people in the West were leaving the Church in large numbers. He complained about the growing doubts of many priests regarding some aspects of Catholic doctrine, especially the real presence of Christ in the eucharist, the eternal virginity of Mary, and the physical resurrection of Christ.

While many welcomed the reforms of the Church, they can also be seen as fulfilling the prophecies of the Fatima message, when the children were told that Satan would take over the Church and factions within it would fight against one another.

The Archbishop of Vienna, Franz König, was the spokesman for Catholic reformers. In an interview he did not hesitate to attack Cardinal Ratzinger's call for a restoration of the old Church. "To put the emphasis on the word *restoration* sounds very much like nostalgia for the past," he said. "The Church of the past regarded everything new in history with anxiety. It felt itself isolated from a world it regarded as evil. The Church must continue to go forward."

Both Ratzinger and König had their supporters, and their conflict split the Church into two camps. The American bishops called Ratzinger "a prophet of doom," using the words of Pope John. On the other hand, the Latin American bishops were on the side of Ratzinger and saw the work of Satan in the opposition, creating an atmosphere of uncertainty and anxiety in the Church. This is reminiscent of the "diplomatic version" of the Third Secret.

In order to put an end to this controversy, Pope John Paul II convened a conference of bishops in 1985 at a monastery in Rome. Perhaps he was influenced by the Fatima revelation itself, which he had read early in 1982. The purpose was to discuss "the effects of the Second Vatican Council on the life of the Catholic Church" and clear the atmosphere of uncertainty and anxiety. Finally it was agreed to compose a definition of Catholic doctrine that would be valid for all believers. Joseph Cardinal Ratzinger was given the job of drafting it, and it was eventually published in 1992.

"I have read it," declared Cardinal Ratzinger, when asked about the Third Secret of Fatima in 1984. Asked the reason for keeping it secret, he replied, "It would add nothing to what a Christian must know . . . [it is about] a radical call for conversion, the absolute seriousness of history, the dangers threatening the faith and life of Christians and therefore the world. If it is not published—at least for the moment—this is to avoid confusing religious prophecy with sensationalism. But the things contained in this Third Secret correspond to what is announced in Scripture and are confirmed by many other Marian apparitions." By making such statements Ratzinger used the secret to support his points of view, without telling us any details about what's in it.

In 1996 Ratzinger had a talk with the German journalist Peter Seewald, which was printed in the book *Salt of the Earth—Christianity and the Catholic Church at the Turn of the Millennium.*

Seewald: Were you disturbed by the prophecy?
R: No.
S: Why?
R: Because it does not say anything that the Christian message does not already contain.
S: But there is something in it about the end of the world, isn't there?
R: I can't say anything about that now. In any case I was not upset by anything terribly frightening.
S: What about specific dates?

R: Again, nothing. But I won't go into further details here and now.

On October 13, 1996, Cardinal Ratzinger took part in the celebrations of the seventy-ninth anniversary of the last apparition of Fatima. The day before, the Catholic broadcasting station interviewed him. He stated, "To all the curious I want to say this: The Holy Virgin is not spreading sensationalism. She does not create fear. She does not present any apocalyptical visions. On the contrary, she leads people to her Son. And that is what is important."

But if that were the case, surely there would have been no reason for so much secrecy. The cardinal said that publishing the Third Secret would bring sensationalism into the Church, but that would be possible only if the contents of the message were, in fact, sensational.

What statements did Pope John Paul II make regarding the secret? He, too, took his time before opening the envelope. During his first journey to Germany in November 1980 a correspondent for a Catholic magazine asked him the question "What has happened to the Third Secret of Fatima? Wasn't it going to be published in 1960?"

The pope answered, "Owing to the seriousness of its contents, in order not to provoke the Communists to take any actions, my predecessors preferred the diplomatic version. Besides that, it is sufficient for every Christian to know the following: When one reads that the oceans will flood entire portions of land, that human beings will die within minutes, and in millions, then one should not desire publication of the secret. Knowledge means responsibility. It is dangerous when someone only wishes to satisfy his curiosity, if he is not prepared to do something about his discoveries, or if he is convinced we can do nothing to prevent the prophesied disasters from happening."

"What will happen to the Church?" was the question from someone else.

"We have to be prepared to suffer" was the reply. "Before long, great trials will require us to sacrifice our lives. Through your prayers and mine it is still possible to diminish this trial, but it is no longer possible to avert it, because only in this way can the Church be effectively renewed. How many times has the renewal of the Church been brought about by blood! It will not be different this time."

This was the first time we heard anything about the Third Secret that referred to another great Flood, like the one in the Bible. However, before this seems too ominous, we must remember that John Paul II spoke these words in 1980, two years before he actually knew the contents of the secret. In 1982 he made a journey to Fatima to thank the Mother of God for saving his life, after he was shot in 1981. At Fatima he met Sister Lúcia. She confided later to Cardinal Oddi that she "had a long talk with the Holy Father, and as a result we both decided not to publish the Third Message, since it could be misunderstood."

The Italian stigmatist Giorgio Bongiovanni requested that Cardinal Oddi ask John Paul II about the Third Secret during an official breakfast meeting they were to have on November 5, 1991. A stigmatist is someone whose hands and feet bleed at the places where Jesus' body was pierced by nails during the crucifixion, so Bongiovanni is considered a holy person by many in the Church.

He received this reply from Oddi: "The Holy Father replied that he had done everything he could for Fatima and did not consider it necessary to intervene any more, since the Third Secret was no longer a secret, because it had already been revealed many times."

These remarks indicated that perhaps the "diplomatic version" contained the truth, for why else would he insist that the contents were already known? However, if the Vatican didn't want to reveal the true contents of the Third Secret yet, then hinting that the Emrich version was genuine was a good way to deflect further interest in the secret, without actually telling a lie.

Pope John Paul II visited Fatima again on May 13, 2000. May 13 is not only the first of the six days on which the Virgin appeared before the children, it is also the day, in 1981, when he was shot, and almost killed, by a Turkish gunman in Saint Peter's Square. The pope, who turned eighty years old on May 20, 2000, believes the Virgin saved his life.

He has already visited the shrine twice before. On one

visit there he left one of the bullets fired at him in the crown of the statue of the Madonna. In 2000 he beatified Jacinta and Francisco.

The surviving member of the threesome, Lúcia dos Santos, is now ninety-three and still lives in the convent near the Portuguese town of Coimbra.

CHAPTER THIRTEEN
THE FATIMA POPE

IN ORDER TO understand whether or not the predictions of Fatima have been fulfilled, we need to return to Rome on that fateful day of May 13, 1981, a little before 5:00 P.M. Every Wednesday afternoon the center of Rome is jammed with traffic, and this Wednesday was no exception. Dozens of tourist buses and hundreds of private cars were trying to inch their way across the bridge that leads to Saint Peter's Square, the center of the Catholic world.

John Paul II was the first pope to give open-air audiences, which made him a kind of pop star of the faith. What had been reserved for the privileged during the days of his predecessors had now become accessible to all. Every Wednesday, unless he was on one of his frequent journeys abroad, the pope received pilgrims at

5:00 P.M., in winter in a hall of the Vatican, in summer in the open square.

Over forty thousand people were waiting for the Holy Father on this warm Wednesday in May. A murmur went through the crowd when the pope's open Jeep appeared. He was standing up in the Jeep holding on to a railing, wearing a white cassock. As the car crept along through the crowds, people pushed forward to touch his outstretched hand. After fifteen minutes the procession had almost reached its destination—the dais with the pope's seat on it. From there he would greet groups of pilgrims, who would be introduced to him by the clergy of their respective countries.

But on this Wednesday afternoon that was not to happen. The pope had just bent down to give a little blond girl a fatherly hug, when exactly at 5:17 P.M. the sounds of shots shattered the joyous atmosphere. A cry of horror and dismay went up from the crowd. The pope trembled and swayed, blood staining his white robe. He sank back, in slow motion, onto the seat of his Jeep.

Surrounded by police, the Jeep pushed through the chaos in the square, past the horrified and hysterical masses, who were fleeing in all directions in case more shots were fired. Finally the car reached the left side of the basilica, where the pope was given first aid. Ten minutes later an ambulance took him to the Catholic University hospital.

The people in Saint Peter's Square were convinced that John Paul II was dead. That was the announcement that news organizations originally sent out all over the world. Police helicopters flew over Saint Peter's Square, and all over Rome the sirens of patrol cars howled. Meanwhile, three surgeons were fighting to save his life. His blood pressure had sunk so low that his pulse was barely perceptible. The operation lasted five hours and twenty minutes. Luckily, the carotid artery had escaped damage by only a small fraction of an inch, and no vital organs had been hurt. The pope was saved. For all concerned it was a miracle.

While millions all over the world prayed for the Holy Father, Vatican Radio announced that the shooter had been arrested. He was a twenty-three-year-old Turkish student, Mehmet Ali Agca. "I forgive him" were the first words of the pontiff, when he regained consciousness after some hours and had been told about the arrest.

The man who had fired the three shots at the pontiff with a Browning HP Parabellum, a very effective combat weapon, was interrogated for hours. To be sure of hitting his target he had aimed at the pope from a squatting position. When those nearby tried to subdue him, he threatened them with his gun. When a young policeman finally reached him, he pressed the trigger once more, but the 9mm pistol had developed a loading defect. When the crowd saw this, they closed in on him, and it was only with great difficulty that the Swiss Guards, who hurried to the spot, managed to prevent them from killing him right there.

At first he denied the deed, and claimed he was a student at the University of Perugia in Italy. But the police established his identity as Ali Agca, a previously convicted terrorist belonging to the national Islamic liberation party, who had murdered the chief editor of a Turkish newspaper in 1979. After his arrest for that crime he managed to escape, and when John Paul II visited Turkey in 1980, he announced his intention to kill the pope.

When the Turkish police searched for him, they came upon evidence that someone was financing him. After the murder of the editor, Agca seemed suddenly to possess a considerable fortune. He was able to travel, unrecognized, all over Europe. Police traced him to Germany, East Germany, Hungary, Bulgaria, France, Spain, Switzerland, and finally Italy. The Italian judiciary was convinced that Agca was working for the Bulgarian secret service, which represented the KGB.

The pope was convinced that the Mother of God had saved him, for if he had not happened to move his body in a particular way while handing the little girl he had embraced back to her parents, the shot would have penetrated his heart.

When John Paul II was released from the hospital on August 14, 1981, the first thing he did was to go to the Crypt of Saint Peter's to pray at the tombs of his predecessors. "I thought there would be one more tomb there, but the Holy Virgin decided otherwise on that thirteenth day of May, the month dedicated to her," he said. But that May 13 was not just another day in the Marian month of

May—it was the sixty-fourth anniversary of Mary's first apparition at Fatima.

During his convalescence at the hospital John Paul II asked one of his close confidants, the Slovak bishop Pavel Hnilica, to bring him the complete documentation regarding Fatima. "I brought him everything," said the bishop later, in an interview with the Catholic monthly *30 Days*. "Some of the texts were originals. He read everything carefully. After he left the hospital, I took a replica of the statue of Our Dear Lady of Fatima to him at Castelgondolfo.

"He ordered a small church to be built in Poland, in a forest bordering on the Soviet Union, and had the statue installed in it. It is there still, exactly where he placed it, with the face of the Holy Virgin directed at the Soviet Union."

When he left the hospital the pontiff said to Bishop Hnilica, "I have finally understood that the only way to save the world from war is to save it from atheism through the conversion of Russia, according to the message of Fatima."

John Paul II now looked upon himself as the Fatima pope, a title that had originally been given to his predecessor Pius XII. He now considered it his duty to fulfill the wishes of the Mother of God as far as possible. He decided to go on pilgrimage to Fatima and meet Sister Lúcia on May 13, 1982, the first anniversary of the assassination attempt. He wanted to prepare for the consecration of Russia and the world to the Immaculate Heart of Mary, which the Lady of Fatima had insisted the Church do, so many years ago.

Before that, sometime early in 1982, he had the Third Secret brought to him from the Holy Office. He opened the envelope sealed by Pope Paul VI in the presence of Cardinal Ratzinger. He consulted a Portuguese clergyman and requested him to translate the text, taking into account all the nuances of the language.

John Paul II arrived in Lisbon early in the afternoon of May 12, 1982. Riding in the "Popemobile" that he had had flown over from Rome, he passed hundreds of thousands of people waving banners. He entered the capital, and went to a cathedral to pray with Franciscans, nuns of various orders, and laypeople. He had a talk with President Eanes at Belén Palace, then left for Fatima in a helicopter.

Over a million people had gathered at the huge esplanade that had been built at the Cova da Íria in front of the magnificent basilica, as well as by the oak, which had meanwhile grown into a mighty tree, now surrounded by an ornamental iron fence. Many of them had arrived the day before, in order to secure a place, and spent the night praying, just as the pilgrims had done sixty-five years before, during the last appearance of the Mother of God.

It was already night when the white helicopter conveying the pope landed near the apparition site. His first destination was the Capelinha, the little chapel that had been built at the wish of the Holy Virgin.

"I have come because on this day, a year ago, an

attempt was made to assassinate the pope, strangely enough, on the anniversary of the first apparition of Fatima on May thirteenth, 1917," he said. "I recognized, in the connection between the dates, a specific call for me to come here; therefore, I am here."

He then greeted the various foreign delegations, each in its native language. Then the pope lit a candle from the flame of the one burning in front of the statue and with it lit the candles in the hands of the cardinals standing nearby. They in turn passed the flame on to those near them. Within minutes the square at Cova da Íria was transformed into a sea of light. John Paul II prayed, while the others recited the rosary.

This ceremony came to an end at 11:30 P.M. and the pope moved on slowly toward the basilica, to perform a mass together with the bishop of Leiria and Fatima. Suddenly there was a commotion. A tall man dressed as a priest had pushed his way into the group of clergymen near the pope. He started insulting the pope loudly, blaming him for the situation of Catholics in Poland, for letting Communism become stronger, and for the Second Vatican Council.

The pope did not see or hear much of this. His secretary and the American bishop, as well as security guards, protected him with their bodies, while the Portuguese police arrested the man. "Down with the pope! Death to Communism!" he shouted in Spanish, as he was taken away. The pope turned slowly toward him and blessed him.

At the police station the man gave his identity as Juan Fernández Krohn, a Spanish priest. They found in his possession a fifteen-inch-long bayonet, with which, according to his own words, he had intended to kill the pope. He confessed to being a follower of the French traditionalist rebel Cardinal Lefèvre, who radically condemned the changes brought about by the Second Vatican Council. The life of the pope had been threatened for a second time on a thirteenth day of May—and again he was saved.

Sister Lúcia, the last of the three seers, had also taken part in the celebrations on May 13, 1982. She had traveled from her convent at Coimbra, under strict security measures. The pope spoke to her alone for almost half an hour. She warned him that, although the consecration of the world as he had performed it was certainly an act of good faith, it was not in accordance with the instructions of the Mother of God, and therefore not valid. John Paul II promised her he would perform the correct ceremony at the earliest possible time.

The following year, on December 8, 1983, he sent a letter to all bishops everywhere, including those of the Orthodox churches, inviting them to join him in consecrating the world to the Immaculate Heart of Mary on March 25, 1984. The letter contained the text of the prayer to be spoken, which he composed after consultation with Sister Lúcia.

The Statue of the Lady of Fatima was flown into Rome especially for this act of consecration. John Paul II had the statue brought to his private chapel, where he spent the nights of March 24 and 25 praying. The next morning it was placed in front of the Basilica of Saint Peter, where he said the prayer he had prepared.

In part of the prayer he said, "Most especially we entrust and consecrate to You those individuals and nations which need this help most," and he added, almost inaudibly, "particularly Russia," and then went on to say, departing from the published text, "Let Your light illuminate particularly those nations whose consecration You Yourself desire." The threat of nuclear war was also addressed. "Protect us from atomic war, from incalculable self-destruction, from every kind of warfare."

Although Russia was mentioned only in a whisper, Sister Lúcia seemed to be finally satisfied. "Is Russia now consecrated?" she was asked later.

"Yes, now it is so," replied Sister Lúcia. "Now we must wait for the miracle. God will keep His word."

What happened during the following years surprised even the most optimistic observers of world politics, and was repeatedly called a modern miracle. Within one year after the solemn Act of Consecration of Russia and the world to the Immaculate Heart of Mary was performed by John Paul II, there were winds of change in the East. Initially called "perestroika" (remodeling) and "glasnost" (transparency), it finally led to the collapse of the Communist dictatorships of the Warsaw Pact. It is certainly premature to talk of a "conversion of Russia," but at least it can be said it has finally ceased to "spread its errors throughout the world."

Within one year after the consecration ceremony, on March 11, 1985, Mikhail Gorbachev became the new secretary general of the Russian Communist party. Later, when he resigned on Christmas Day 1991, he declared that "fate determined that I should find myself at the top of the state, and it was soon clear to me that something was going wrong in this country. We had much, but we still lived in a much poorer condition than the people in the other industrialized countries. All the halfhearted reforms, of which there were so many, had fallen through. The country was getting nowhere. We had to change everything radically. I was well aware that a reform of this kind in a society like ours would be an extremely difficult and even dangerous undertaking. But today I am convinced that the democratic revolution, which we began in the spring of 1985, was historically the correct step."

Russia's conversion from a Communist superpower to a more open society, embracing religion, was a miracle in itself. In 1979, as the KGB files that were handed over to the Italian government in November 1999 show, Russia's attitude toward the pope was quite severe, advocating extreme measures against the pontiff. In a memorandum dated November 13, 1979, the KGB were advised to "take all possible measures against the Polish pope—if necessary, using additional measures beyond disinformation and discrediting him." The reference to "additional measures" is understood to mean "not excluding physical elimination." As the documents revealed, the KGB even planted a recording device within the Madonna statue of the Vatican secretary of state.

After their release the Italian press cited the papers as evidence that the KGB gave to the Bulgarian Secret Service the original order for the assassination of John Paul II that was attempted by their agent Ali Agca.

In 1987 democracy began in the USSR, with the repeal of sanctions against religion. Religious leaders and personalities, like Mother Teresa from Calcutta, were allowed to visit the country. An influential newspaper of the Soviet intelligentsia, which at one time would have been strictly secular, backed the cause of the Christian pilgrims who streamed to the village of Hrushiv in the Ukraine, where Marian apparitions had occurred.

On the morning of April 26, 1987, the anniversary of the Chernobyl catastrophe, Marina Kisin, a twelve-year-old farmer's daughter, left home to go to school. Diagonally opposite her house stood a dilapidated church, plundered by the Communists and now nailed shut. Suddenly Marina noticed a strange light hovering above the church. When she went closer to the light, out of curiosity, she recognized a woman, dressed in black robes of mourning, holding a child in her arms. Then she heard a voice which told her that the Ukrainians, on account of all their sufferings, had been chosen to lead the Soviet Union back to Christianity.

Marina was frightened and ran back home as fast as

she could, to tell her mother and sister about her mysterious encounter. Minutes later all three of them hurried to the scene of the vision, where the light and the mysterious figure in black could still be seen. The figure nodded to them as if in greeting, and Marina's mother, Miroslava, fell on her knees devoutly. "That is the Virgin Mary," she hissed to her daughters. "Kneel down and pray!"

Within hours news of the occurrence had spread and people started coming to the place. Soon pilgrims came from thousands of miles away, from Georgia and the Baltic states. The main difference between Fatima and Hrushiv was that here it was not only Marina who saw the Mother of God; half the pilgrims who came saw her, too, sometimes clearly, sometimes as a shadow.

Some of them heard her message as well. "Oh, my daughter Ukraine, I have come to you, for you have suffered most, and during all your trials you have preserved your faith in the Most Holy Heart. I have come to you, so that you may go forth to convert Russia. Pray for Russia! Pray for that lost Russian nation. For if Russia does not accept Christ, a third world war is unavoidable."

One of the half million pilgrims who went to Hrushiv was the Catholic activist Josip Terelya, who had spent twenty years in Russian prison camps, and shortly before had been released on Gorbachev's orders. He said, "The glow around the chapel was now about six hundred feet high. The entire area was enveloped in a light that was somehow heavenly and breathtaking. It was something between the silvery luster of the moon and the glow of a fluorescent lamp.

"In the light above the church there was a smaller, more intense light, that looked like a bright globe. It was a fiery ball that moved back and forth, and when it was above the chapel, it was a silvery lilac color. It swayed forward and backward, shimmering. Then it moved to the left and finally descended onto the main dome of the church. The Virgin Mary took form in the sphere, as if she had been conveyed into our reality by the globe, acting as a vehicle. It was as if the light was being shown by a projector from somewhere very far away."

Again, as in the Fatima visions, we have a UFO-like image of the Virgin's "vehicle."

On the first three days the apparition was dressed in a robe of flaming colors. Others saw her differently. Some saw her with a crown on her head, others with a ring in her hand. But when she was dressed in black, and held the child in her arms, everyone saw the same thing.

This was not like Fatima, where her appearances were limited to certain times. The Virgin appeared many times during the day. Not everyone could see her, and even some priests and nuns could not witness her appearance. But more than half of those present could catch at least a glimpse of her.

This was also experienced by observers from the KGB and the militia, who, at the beginning, had tried to photograph everyone who visited the scene of the vision. They knelt down when the vision began, "so as not to be conspicuous," and when they saw it, one of them called out loud enough for everyone to hear, "There is a God!" An officer of the militia, who was supposed to guard the church, took off his cap and tore the insignia from his uniform. "What can I do, when I have seen the Mother of God?" he declared. Two weeks later he was sent by his department for psychiatric treatment.

Another officer, who had too much to drink, drew his pistol and fired a shot at the vision. Many witnesses saw a beam of light go out from the Virgin and touch him. The officer fell to the ground unconscious, and the arm that had fired had turned black, as if it had suffered a very strong electric shock. On May 12 a television team from Kiev made a film of the scene. When the film was shown the next day, on the seventy-fourth anniversary of Fatima, thousands of viewers could see the Mother of God on their TV screens.

After the middle of May the daily appearances became paler, and after four weeks they could no longer be seen. But there were appearances at thirteen other places in the Communist world, mostly at destroyed monasteries and closed-down churches. Again and again the Mother of God warned the people about the danger of a third world war, and appealed to them to repent and convert, in order to avoid it.

When John Paul II heard about the vision at Hrushiv, he saw in it a sign of hope, that the miracle of the conversion of Russia would at last become true. On November 7, 1987 he received Josip Terelya, who had meanwhile been allowed to travel out of the Soviet Union. The private audience lasted forty-three minutes, during which the pontiff found out about the situation of Catholics in the Ukraine as well as about the apparitions.

On April 29, 1988, a meeting took place at the grandiose Catherine Hall of the Kremlin between Mikhail Gorbachev, the Russian Orthodox patriarch of Moscow, and five metropolitan bishops. Only five years before such a meeting would have been unthinkable. Gorbachev announced a new law regarding freedom of religion. "Believers are Soviet citizens, workers, patriots," he said. "They have the right to express their convictions with dignity."

Communist regimes began to fall like dominoes, and the wall between East and West Germany was torn down. "What is now happening in the East has such astonishing and unexpected dimensions and is happening so fast, that one can only say that the hand of God is behind it," commented the French professor of philosophy Marcel Clément. "Extraordinary promises were made at Fatima. The present events do not yet prove that the prophecy has been fulfilled, but they make it appear that it is possible. Everything depends on how seriously the matter of religious freedom is taken under the new circumstances."

The French *Le Figaro* columnist F. Foussard said, "It appears in no way illogical to assume that what is happening in the East could be the result of the promises of Fatima. It is obvious to me that a kind of miracle is happening. Moreover, no one can give a purely rational and political explanation for what is occurring."

Six months later, on May 12, 1991, the pope journeyed to Fatima for a second time. On the next day, which was the anniversary of both the first apparition and the day when his life was saved, John Paul II solemnly repeated the consecration of the world.

Russia sent a very special person to the ceremony. Gennadii Gerasimov had been the spokesman for the foreign ministry under Gorbachev, before he was appointed ambassador to Portugal. He told a Lisbon newspaper that this was his third visit to the shrine. He also conceded that in his house, hanging on the wall, he had an icon of the Holy Mother of Kazan, the protecting patroness of Russia, a confession one would never have expected from a Soviet ambassador only a few years before.

During the next few months progress in the Soviet Union could no longer be held back. During the early hours of August 19, the anniversary, once again, of a Fatima apparition, Communist hardliners staged a coup against President Gorbachev, who was held prisoner at his country villa in Crimea. It was the final blow in the death of Communism there.

Boris Yeltsin, president of the Russian Republic, took a stand against the leaders of the coup. Gorbachev was driven from his office as president of the Soviet Union, a country which had ceased to exist by the time the new year began.

During the night of December 31, 1991, there was an atmosphere of excitement in Moscow's Red Square. Thousands of people gathered in front of the Kremlin, where they sang ballads, danced, and drank wine, vodka, or Crimean champagne. In spite of the biting cold of the Russian winter they were filled with joy, because it was the last day of the Soviet Union.

While the boisterous crowd was celebrating, a man rushed forward toward the Lenin Mausoleum, carrying a statue of Our Lady of Fatima. He lifted it up high, in a gesture of victory.

When the pope saw pictures of this memorable night, his eyes filled with tears. "The pope saw the turmoil in the Soviet Union as a kind of mystery play," wrote Bernstein and Politi in their biography, *His Holiness,* "in which, in his opinion, our dear Lady of Fatima played a major role."

Two years later John Paul II told the Italian journalist Vittorio Messori, "And what about the three Portuguese children of Fatima, who unexpectedly and shortly before the outbreak of the October revolution heard, 'Russia will return' and 'in the end my Heart will triumph'? It is impossible that they could have invented such statements. They were ignorant of history and geography, knew even less about social movements and ideological developments. And yet, what they announced is exactly what has happened."

CHAPTER FOURTEEN
VISIONS OF MARY

THERE HAVE BEEN Marian apparitions throughout the history of Christianity. In August in the year 363 the Mother of God appeared to a married couple in Rome and asked for a church to be built at a spot where they would find snow the next morning—a miracle indeed, in the heat of an Italian summer—but the patch of snow was found and the church built there, the Santa Maria Maggiore, which is today one of the most important shrines of the Eternal City.

During the year 1026 the Holy Virgin appeared to Saint Fulbert, who later built the famous cathedral of Chartres in France. In 1465 an apparition of Mary taught Alanus de Rupé Paris the prayers of the rosary.

And in 1531 the apparitions of María on the Tepeyac hill in Mexico led to mass conversions. Twelve years had passed since the bloody conquest of the Aztec empire of Mexico by the unscrupulous adventurer Hernando Cortés, who succeeded in destroying within days a culture that had flourished for centuries. He ordered the demolition of the temple pyramids of the Aztecs and the building of Catholic churches all over the land.

In 1528 the emperor also appointed a committee of five officials to administer the conquered territories in Mexico. The head of the committee was Don Nuño de Guzmán, who soon revealed himself to be a remorseless tyrant and oppressor. Guzmán tried to justify his violent treatment of the Indians and their enslavement by saying that the Aztecs were creatures without souls, related to the monsters mentioned in ancient legends. To convert them would be a waste of time and effort, and he felt it was quite proper to exploit them.

The Aztec Juan Diego from the village of Cuautitlán and his uncle Juan Bernardino from the village of Toltpetlac were among the first Indians who let themselves be baptized, and they regularly visited the church to receive religious instruction. After his wife died in 1529, Juan Diego went to stay with his uncle at Tolpetlac. Early at dawn on December 9 he started out on his way to the church. The way led over the Tepeyac hill on which had stood, during Aztec days, a temple of the earth goddess Tonantzín. It was now in ruins.

When he had almost reached the top of the hill, he became aware of a melody in the silence of the morning. It seemed to come from a bright white cloud that was floating above the top of the hill, surrounded by rays of blinding light in all the colors of the rainbow. As the melody died down he heard a tender voice that called out to him lovingly, using the affectionate form of his name, "Juanito, Juan Diegito!"

He hurried to the top of the hill to stand face to face with a breathtakingly beautiful lady, who gave him a friendly smile. Her robes shone bright as the sun and the rays of light that went out from her pierced through the bushes and the rocks. Everything around him was sparkling with the colors that she radiated. She said, "My dearest little son, know that I am the Virgin Mary, the Mother of God, who is the Lord of everything in heaven and on earth. I want a temple to be built here for me, where I can show and give my help and my protection to all those who love me, who call out to me and trust me. Go to the house of the bishop in the city of Mexico, tell him that I have sent you and that I want a temple to be built here. Tell him what you have seen." The conversation was carried out in Nahuatl, the flowery language of the Aztecs, which is full of terms of affection.

Juan Diego hurried off by the quickest way to Mexico City. He entered the city while most of the people there were still sleeping and went straight to the house of Bishop Zumárraga.

Juan hammered on the big doors of the bishop's residence. A servant slowly opened the heavy wooden doors and inspected the poorly dressed peasant with suspicion.

When Juan politely expressed his wish to see the bishop, the servant told him to sit in the courtyard and wait.

After an hour or so the servant called him and said that His Excellency was ready to receive him. Since the bishop spoke only Spanish and Juan only Nahuatl, an interpreter, the well-educated Spaniard Juan Gonzáles, was called to help. The Aztec told them his story. "I must think over what you said, and then decide what to do," said the bishop eventually. Then, seeing Juan's obvious disappointment, he laid his hand on his shoulder in a fatherly gesture and said, "You must come back here when I have more time."

And with that he waved him out of the room. Juan left, followed by the mocking grins of the guards who had been watching the whole scene with amusement. Feeling small and disappointed, the Aztec went home. As he crossed the Tepeyac hill, he saw that the beautiful lady was waiting for him. "It's clear that the bishop thinks I have invented the story," he complained to her. "You must send a more important person next time."

But the Madonna replied, "Listen, my dear son, it is very important that it is you who goes to the bishop. I therefore order you to go there again tomorrow morning."

The next morning he did what he had been told to do. He met the bishop, went down on his knees, and wept and pleaded with him to fulfill the wish of the Holy Virgin. But the bishop answered rather condescendingly, "I can't order a church to be built based on just one person's word. You must bring me proof that you have been personally sent by the Holy Virgin." With that the bishop thought the matter was at an end.

When he reached home Diego found his uncle seriously ill. He called for the village healer but he could not help. He then decided to fetch the priest the next morning from Mexico City, to give his uncle the last sacrament. When he came to the Tepeyac hill he decided to take a detour, so the Lady could not see him. But she suddenly appeared in front of him. "What has happened, my little son, where are you going to?" she asked him.

"My uncle is very ill and will die soon. I'm going to Mexico City to bring a priest."

"Don't worry about the sickness of your uncle, he will not die. Believe me, he is already healed," she told him.

And in fact, as Juan Diego later learned, at that very moment his uncle had been cured. Then the Queen of the Heavens told Juan to go to the top of the hill, gather the flowers that were growing there, and bring them to her.

"Flowers in winter?" Juan asked himself, but nothing surprised him anymore. And indeed, when he reached the top of the hill he was astounded by the number and variety of beautiful flowers that were growing there, where only the day before there had been nothing but naked rock, thorny bushes, and cacti. He gathered a pile of flowers, laid them on his cloak, and carried them to the Mother of God, who was waiting for him down below.

"The flowers are the proof you should carry to the

bishop," she told him. "But do not show them to anyone but him."

Juan hurried to the city and went to the house of the bishop, but the guards wouldn't let him in. Other servants, seeing him waiting outside in the cold, came out to tease him. "Now, what have you got in that cloak?" they asked, and jostled him. Soon they discovered that Juan had brought flowers. They tried to grab them, but it seemed as if the flowers had been painted onto the cloak, so that they could not be picked up. Amazed by this, they ran to the bishop and told him what they had seen.

Bishop Zumárraga ordered Juan to be brought to him. "You have the proof I have asked for?" he said. Juan opened his cloak to lay the flowers at the feet of the bishop. But as the sweet smelling flowers fell to the ground, they dissolved into the air and disappeared. At the same time the portrait of the Lady appeared on his cloak, just as he had seen her on Tepeyac hill. The astonished bishop jumped up from his seat and knelt down before the miraculous image. He then carefully untied the cloak from Juan's neck and shoulders and carried it to his private chapel.

"Yes, I will build a church for the Queen of Heaven!" the bishop promised, and asked Juan to lead him to the Tepeyac hill. The next day the bishop went with Juan to visit his uncle, who was now in good health. The Virgin had visited Juan Bernardino earlier and told him this prediction: "Your nephew will come with the bishop. When they arrive, tell the bishop I wish to be revered in the shrine as the Holy Mary, the Coatlaxopeuh." The last was a word in Nahuatl, meaning "the one who crushes the snake." But it was unknown to the interpreter. He thought that the Indian meant Guadalupe, the well-known place of pilgrimage in Spain. Due to this misunderstanding the Lady of Mount Tepeyac received the title "Holy Virgin of Guadalupe."

When the miraculous image of the Virgin of Guadalupe was exhibited at the cathedral of Mexico City, people came in hundreds and thousands to see it. On December 26, 1531, the miraculous portrait of Mary was carried in a triumphal procession to a chapel built on the Tepeyac hill.

She had one foot on the crescent moon, which for the Aztecs was a sign of her victory over their god Quetzalcoatl (the plumed serpent), since the crescent was his symbol. The blue-green color of her cloak was the color worn by the Aztec kings, which meant that she was a queen. The tassels under her hands were like those that pregnant Aztec women wore, so she was therefore a mother. The stars and constellations on her cloak showed that she was the Queen of Heaven.

The chapel was made larger between 1600 and 1620, and finally in 1694 a large basilica was built, which from then on housed the miraculous image. Due to the danger of collapse the old basilica had to be closed during the 1970s, and a huge modern basilica has been built next to it, with seating for ten thousand people. Every year over twenty million pilgrims visit there, walking on their knees on the stones leading up to it.

The biggest miracle is the cloak itself. Usually the agave fibers, out of which the cloak was made, have a life span of about twenty years. But even after 466 years it does not show any sign of decay. The soot from the millions of candles that had been burned at the foot of the portrait before it was enclosed in a glass case does not seem to have affected the portrait at all. The colors look as fresh as if they had just been painted.

As for the composition of the colors themselves, laboratory tests of a piece of the cloth carried out by Nobel prize winner Richard Kuhn of Heidelberg, in 1936, revealed that the paint was of neither vegetable nor animal nor mineral origin. A microscopic examination carried out ten years later did not show any signs of a brush having been used.

Professor Francisco Campos Rivera repeated this investigation in 1954 and 1966, each time using the most modern microscopes, and came to the same conclusion. The miraculous portrait is not a painting at all. In this way it is similar to the famous Shroud of Turin, in Italy, which is supposed to be the burial cloth of Jesus.

In 1929, when the professional photographer Alfonso Gonzáles made enlargements of various pictures he had shot of the image, he discovered human faces reflected in the eyes of the virgin. In 1951 the graphics expert Carlos Salinas took up the investigation. He examined the eyes and found in the right eye the reflection of the face of a man with a beard. Salinas told the archbishop of Mexico City about this and he set up a committee to investigate it further.

Experts found that the bearded face looked like the oldest known portrait of Juan Diego.

In July 1956 two oculists, Dr. Javier Torroello Bueno and Dr. Raphael Torifa Lavoignet, examined the pictures and noted light reflections typical of ocular reflections in the eyes. "The position of the reflected image in the eye and its distortion are typical of reflections produced in a normal human eye," they reported. "When the light from an ophthalmoscope is directed at the pupil of a human eye, we see a reflection in the outer circle. With the correct lens it is possible to see an image at the back of the eye. When this instrument is directed at the eye in the portrait of the Madonna, light is reflected in a similar manner."

In other words, at the moment of the miracle, the cloak acted like a photographic negative, again like the Shroud of Turin. It must have been exposed at the moment when the Madonna first appeared on the cloak, because Juan Diego's face was reflected by her eye.

A further investigation, carried out by the oculist Dr. C. Wahlig and his wife, an optician, revealed more faces in the eyes of the Madonna—those of the bishop and his interpreter and also a crouching figure in a corner, who was probably a servant.

No artist could have painted the eyes so perfectly, for the principles governing ocular reflections were discovered only during the last twenty years of the nineteenth century. Said Wahlig, "It was as if it was part of the plan to present the picture of the Mother of God to the people of our time as a scientifically provable phenomenon."

The scientific proof was confirmed when, in 1963, the management of Kodak, after a thorough investigation, announced that the picture was a photograph. In May 1979 the American scientists Professor Philip Callahan and Professor Jody Smith of the University of Florida made infrared photographs of the cloak. Since pigments absorb and reflect infrared light in varying degrees, such pictures can reveal alterations and areas that have been painted over. In the majority of the image close-up infrared shots reveal no brushstrokes. On the other hand, areas that were known to have been painted over in the past—for instance, the hands of the Madonna were made smaller to make them look more Mexican—showed all the usual characteristics of normal painting techniques.

Professor Callahan finally stated, "It may sound strange when a scientist says something like this, but I for my part have to say it. The original picture is a miracle."

Another amazing detail is that the stars on the cloak of the Madonna exactly reflect the constellations as seen in the sky above Mexico City on December 12, 1531, at dawn, but in reverse order like a mirror image.

The next major Marian miracles took place in France. It was a hot summer day in the French Alps on September 19, 1846, when, on the slopes of the high, lonely valley of La Salette, two children were grazing their herd of sheep. When we think of Fatima this story begins to seem familiar.

The children, a girl and a boy, had met each other for

the first time only two days before. Mélanie Calvat, fifteen years old, the daughter of a poorly paid sawmill worker, had herded sheep since she was eight years old to earn money for her family. Maximin Giraud had just turned eleven, and had only begun herding sheep on September 17, to fill in for a sick shepherd. His father was also poor, with earnings too small to feed his family. Neither of them could read or write, and they had no religious education. They could speak only the local dialect.

After hours of driving their sheep they had at last reached their destination, the top of a nearby hill, with a good meadow on it. They admired the grand panorama offered by the majestic mountain peaks around them. They played for some time, building towers with the stones that lay around, then ate their sparse lunches of bread and cheese. After that they lay down and dozed for a while.

When they woke up at about three o'clock in the afternoon, they were shocked to find that their herds of sheep had vanished. They jumped up at once and went in search of them. But when Mélanie happened to glance at the spot where they had been resting, she saw a light, brighter than the sun. A huge ball of fire was floating in the air above the earth.

Maximin and Mélanie cried out in fear when they felt a blast of air that came out from the sphere. At first they wanted to run, then they picked up sticks, intending to drive it away. But soon they were filled with a feeling of joy and reverence. They stood still and stared at the ball of light, which was about fifteen feet in diameter. Inside the sphere they saw an even brighter sphere of light that seemed to be moving (this is reminiscent of the "wheel within a wheel" seen by Ezekiel in the Old Testament). Within that they saw a very beautiful lady of pure light, sitting on the little tower of rocks they had built.

She hid her face in her hands, as if she were crying, then stood up slowly while the tears ran down her cheeks. She wore a strange costume and a bonnet of lace that was surrounded by a wreath of shining, fiery red roses. On her neck she wore a crucifix on which a crucified figure, covered with blood, seemed to be alive and suffering in the throes of death. She then turned to the children who were staring at her.

"Don't be afraid," she said. "I have come to give you a great message."

The Lady spoke pure French. When the children, who spoke only the local dialect, could not grasp everything she said, she repeated what she had said in words they could understand. "There will be a great famine. The great ones will suffer from hunger and repent. The nuts will go bad and the grapes will start rotting." At that moment Mélanie noticed that the lips of the Lady of light were moving but that she could not hear what was being said. This happened when she was telling a particular secret to Maximin alone. A little while later she spoke to Mélanie without Maximin being able to hear.

After that Mélanie and Maximin could both hear

everything. "If they change their ways, the mountains will turn into bread and the earth will be covered with potatoes." She then asked them, "Do you say your prayers, my children?"

"No, good Lady, not all the time," they both replied honestly, a bit embarrassed.

"But, my children, you should pray regularly every evening. If you can't do more, say at least the Lord's Prayer and Ave Maria." She asked them one more question. "Haven't you seen rotting grain, my children?" Both denied that.

But the bright Lady knew better and she reminded Maximin that a while ago his father had shown him some rotting ears of corn. He remembered the incident and asked himself, *Does the Lady know everything?*

"Well, my children, you will tell all my people what I have said to you!" said the Lady, closing the conversation. She then went past the children, still surrounded by light, went up to the top of a small hill, floated above it about four feet from the ground, and began to vanish slowly. Her head, then her shoulders, then her body, finally her shoes dissolved into thin air. When Mélanie, who had run behind her, tried to grab one of her roses, she found nothing in her hand. There was a glow of light about fifteen feet above them, that lasted for several more minutes, then the apparition was over.

When the children went home, they told everyone about the mysterious apparition with all the details. A priest, Abbé Lagier, heard about the incident. He visited the children, questioned them, and came to the conclusion that two such simple shepherd children could not have invented the story. Soon pilgrims started coming to visit the site, although at first the bishop opposed it. When the bishop of Grenoble set up an official committee to investigate the events on July 19, 1847, over three hundred thousand pilgrims had already visited the apparition site. At the end of the investigation, which lasted for three months, he was sure that the children hadn't lied or had hallucinations.

What impressed everyone the most was that Mélanie and Maximin could repeat the message of the Virgin from memory in perfect French, although it was a language they had never spoken and could understand only a little. The conclusion of the committee was further supported by two cases of miraculous healing.

Twelve years after La Salette, in 1858, the Holy Virgin appeared to the peasant girl Bernadette Soubirous at Lourdes in France.

Bernadette's family was poor, so poor that they had to live in the rotting rooms of the former village prison. Fourteen-year-old Bernadette was a sick girl who suffered from asthma and the aftereffects of cholera, which she had contracted as a ten-year-old child.

It all began on February 11, 1858, when she went with her brothers and sisters and her cousin to gather firewood. She heard a noise and suddenly saw a golden cloud in a grotto on the banks of the River Gave, and shortly after that she saw a young and beautiful lady, who smiled at Bernadette. Bernadette automatically grabbed her rosary and started praying, and the lady joined in before disappearing.

Bernadette told her family about this event but nobody believed her. Her mother did not allow her to return to the place with the other girls for three days. She gave one of the girls some holy water, so that if the apparition occurred again, she could sprinkle it with the water and see whether the devil was involved.

The Lady, when she appeared again, reacted to this test with a smile. On February 18 a prominent woman from the village accompanied Bernadette to the grotto, along with her children, and they all saw the visitor when she appeared again.

"Give me the joy of seeing you daily for fourteen days," the Lady told Bernadette. Bernadette fulfilled this wish and was accompanied by more and more people on each occasion when she went to the grotto.

"Pray for the poor sinners, pray for the sick world!" was the message that the White Lady gave her again and again. After the sixth apparition the police commissioner of the village took action. He interrogated the girl for hours and tried to get her to contradict herself. Afterward her father forbade her to go to the grotto, but then changed his mind the next day.

During the next apparition the Lady asked Bernadette to have a chapel built for her at the spot and promised to provide a spring with healing waters. During the ninth apparition, on February 25, Bernadette started digging in the moist earth in front of the grotto. Soon a spring flowed out, which is still flowing today. The next day the first healing occurred, when a man was cured of an eye disease.

During the fifteenth apparition, on March 4, there were at least twenty-three thousand people present. When the sixteenth apparition occurred on March 25, the Lady identified herself. When she revealed her name to Bernadette, she did not understand it. The village priest asked her later, "Is it therefore the most Holy Virgin that you see?"

But she answered, "No, it is the Immaculate Conception." The girl had never heard this title before and did not know that it referred to the Virgin Mary. After the seventeenth apparition the opposition struck. Bernadette was taken to a psychiatric clinic, the spring was declared to be merely a mineral spring, and the grotto was blocked to prevent entry. After she was released from the clinic, Bernadette saw the Lady for the last time on July 16.

On July 28 the bishop of Tarbes set up a committee to investigate the apparitions. Three years later he announced in a pastoral letter that he considered Bernadette's visions to be genuine, and the grotto of Masabielle became the most famous place of pilgrimage in the Christian world. In 1866 Bernadette joined a convent. She died in 1879, after which her corpse did not show any signs of decay. She was beatified in 1925.

Over five million pilgrims visit Lourdes every year, where they can see the body of Bernadette lying in a glass coffin. Over five thousand cases of healing have been reported, of which sixty-four have been recognized by the Church as being miracles.

CHAPTER FIFTEEN
SIGNS IN THE SKY

MANY MARIAN VISIONS have taken place since Fatima, and still occur today, even right here in the United States. According to the comprehensive list of apparitions compiled in 1933 by Gottfried Hierzenberger and Otto Nedomansky, who looked at data for over 900 cases, there were, at that time, 31 apparitions in the eighteenth century, 105 in the nineteenth century, and 430 in the twentieth century.

Marian apparitions increased greatly after the Fatima visions in 1917. In the decade of 1920–29 there were 16 cases; in 1930–39, 40 cases; 1940–49, 59 cases; 1950–59, 76 cases; 1960–69, 376 cases; 1970–79, 51 cases; and in 1980–89 there were 122 cases. Many of these Marian appearances included bright, multicolored lights and whirling, UFO-like disks. People were given prophecies, often about upcoming wars.

Many apparitions have asked that statues of the Madonna be made, and many of these have later seemed to "weep." In 1977 in Cairo, Egypt, a statue sweated oil. On September 21, 1982, in Italy, a statue of the Virgin wept tears of blood that tested as being from the AB blood group. On September 8, 1984, a Belgian Madonna wept tears of blood. On September 16 of that year a Colombian photo of a Madonna statue seemed to cry bloody tears.

On August 8, 1983, also in Belgium, a Madonna statue wept tears of water. This also happened on May 19, 1984, in Brooklyn, New York, and on June 29 of that same year in Chicago. Madonna statues wept in Canada on June 17, 1986, and on July 13, 1987.

Other kinds of signs have been given as well. On September 8, 1954, in Austria, the six-year-old peasant girl Annemarie Lex was playing in the farmyard next to her house. Shortly after 3:00 P.M. the little girl ran to the kitchen and told her mother Aloisia, "Mama, the Virgin was in the garden, completely snow-white, and had a long rosary with a big cross on it. There was a golden buckle on her belt and she had a white veil. She just stood and smiled and did not speak. When the wind moved her veil, I could see beautiful curls!" Naturally, her mother didn't believe her. Only after the girl repeated her story again and again, without contradictions, did Aloisia start to believe her.

"A ball of light came with a stormy wind and the hens all stood in a row, as if they were paralyzed," Annemarie said. "I was afraid and wanted to run away but my feet wouldn't move."

On October 13, 1955, Annemarie's mother went into the garden to pray in front of a holy picture, which she had attached to a tree not far from the spot where her daughter claimed to have seen the Madonna. Although she was partially paralyzed on the left side after a difficult childbirth, and was bedridden most of the time, Aloisia was trying as best she could to run the household.

While she was praying, she suddenly saw a white figure approaching her, stopping at the spot where her daughter had had her vision. At first Aloisia thought someone from the village was playing a joke on her (Annemarie's story had gotten around quickly), and she called out to her family. At that moment the figure disappeared. A year later, on September 6, 1956, she had a vision of Christ while she was ill and lying in bed. She was immediately healed.

Soon after that, when she went out into the garden again, she noticed something strange. At the place where she and her daughter had seen the apparitions, the grass was drying out in the form of a cross about four feet long and about two and a half feet across. The cross on the lawn became a matter of dispute in the village. When the neighbors expressed their suspicions that the family itself had created the cross, the chief inspector of the local police, Gendarm Neunherz, ordered it to be watched day and night. He eventually became convinced it was genuine.

The bishop had the cross fenced off, and interrogated the members of the family. Samples of the ground and grass were sent to the Botanical Institute in Vienna. The results, published on October 23, 1956, said, "Through comparative growing experiments it has been shown that within the outline of the cross there are no chemical changes in the ground that would have a negative effect on plant growth. Spraying the lawn with weed killer could not have made such a sharp delineation." Only a veto from the local priest prevented it from being recognized by the Church as a miracle.

Although Church officials rejected it, thousands of pilgrims came to the village to see the cross. More than once, during the spring and summer of 1968, there were solar miracles as well.

In 1968, Dr. Neubauer of the University of Innsbruck made a psychological examination of Frau Lex. He found her to be "a typical person of her social class, sober and firmly rooted in reality, who did not exhibit any extraordinary psychological aspects." Nevertheless, on April 12, 1969, the archbishop declared, "There is no justification for considering this natural phenomenon to be a supernatural intervention."

After Aloisia Lex died in 1983, her relatives did not take care of the cross, so now grass has grown over it and it is no longer visible.

This was not the only case of a cross appearing in the

grass. Three more appeared in Austria between 1966 and 1980. Another appeared in Germany on July 19, 1972, that was ten feet long and five feet wide.

On June 18, 1961, in Garabandal, Spain, four little girls, ages eleven and twelve, had a special kind of Marian sighting. They were playing on the village square near the church in the evening, when they heard a clap of thunder, and before them stood what they described as a "figure of great beauty surrounded by a glowing light, which was, however, not blinding." The girls stared at the visitor in silent astonishment, then it disappeared. On June 20, when the four girls were together again, the brilliant light appeared again for a few seconds, at 8:30 P.M., exactly the same time as before.

The next day the four children went to the same place at the same time, hoping that the apparition would reappear. A vision came that could be seen only by the children. Others who were present saw the girls go into a trance and look upward, as their bodies stiffened and their features became transformed by a supernatural glow. This vision repeated itself during the next two days.

The apparitions always followed the same pattern. The girls felt an inner call, a feeling of great joy, and set off toward the apparition site. The calls were timed so that all four girls, no matter where they were, arrived at the spot at exactly the same moment. As if reacting to a command, all four of them fell into a trance at the same time. Their bodies stiffened, and they became immune to all external influences. People poked needles into them, held burning candles under their arms, and shone bright lights directly in their eyes, but the girls did not even bat their eyelashes.

The girls have been told that an announcement is coming in the future, "which everyone will be able to understand." It will be something that happens in the atmosphere, "like two colliding stars," but no one will be physically harmed by it. It will take the shape of a cross, and has to do with a word that starts with the letter *A* in Spanish. One of the girls believes that it will suddenly stop a third world war that will have broken out.

The girls will announce the miracle eight days before it happens so that sick people can come to the place where the apparition will occur, because everyone who experiences the miracle will be healed.

The miracle will happen at Garabandal, at an elevated spot at which tall pine trees grow. It will be visible from the hills all around, and look like a pillar of smoke or fire. People will be able to see it and photograph it. One girl says she has been told the exact date, but since she is allowed to announce it only eight days before it happens, she is only able to give us hints. It will happen on a Thursday evening, between the seventh and the seventeenth days of a month between February and July, at 8:30 P.M., and will last for about a quarter of an hour. Once she was drawn into saying it will be in April, and she is reported to have said it will happen after the pope goes to Russia.

It is possible that this prophecy refers to the comets

Hyakutake and Hale-Bopp, which were visible in the northern sky in the spring of 1996. If we draw an imaginary line, tracing their courses through the sky, they form a perfect cross, and their paths crossed on April 11, which was a Thursday. "Two colliding stars," "visible to everyone," seems to fit to this astronomical event. However, the girls believe the miracle hasn't happened yet.

When Pope John XXIII died, one of the girls, Conchita, told her mother that there will be three more popes. Asked how she knew this, the seer replied, "From the Holy Virgin. Actually there will be four, but she does not count one." When asked why that was, Conchita replied, "She didn't say why, only that she wasn't counting one. But she also said that one would reign for a very short period."

After John XXIII there have been three popes: Paul VI (1963–78), John Paul I (1978), and John Paul II (who has been pope since 1978). Already the prediction that one would reign for a very short period has been fulfilled with John Paul I, whose pontificate lasted for only thirty-three days. This would mean that John Paul II is the last pope.

That matches an old prophecy of Saint Malachy, a bishop in Ireland who was born in 1094 and died in 1148. His prophecies were printed for the first time in 1585. We have no way of knowing whether they were truly written by Saint Malachy, or have only been attributed to him. But one thing is certain: whoever wrote them predicted the future of the popes with extreme accuracy.

In this prophecy 112 popes are named, starting with

Celestin II (1143–1144), with short descriptions, which apply either to their characters or their aims or to the periods of their reign. It is amazing how accurate these are.

"Religio depopulata," the "depopulated religion," was the description given for Pope Benedict XV (1914–22). During his pontificate there was a general reduction of the Christian population in Europe, owing to the First World War and the Spanish influenza, as well as bloody revolutions.

"Fides intrepida," "unshakable faith," was the description for Pius XI (1922–39). During his reign the Church had to withstand the persecutions of Hitler and Stalin.

"Pastor angelicus," the "angelic shepherd," was the name for Pius XII (1939–1958), for whom the "miracle of the sun" of Fatima was repeated in the Vatican gardens. He proclaimed the dogma of the bodily ascension of Mary into heaven and consecrated the whole world to her.

"Pastor et nauta," "shepherd and seafarer," applied to John XXIII (1958–63), who came from the shepherds' village of Soto-il-Monte near Bergamo, and herded sheep as a boy. Before being elected pope he had been patriarch of the famous seafaring city of Venice.

"Flos florum," "flower of the flowers," was Paul VI (1963–1978), who had three lilies on his coat of arms.

"De medietate lunae," "from the half moon," refers to the birth name of John Paul I (1978), Albino Luciani (which means "lunar"). He was elected pope during the

time of the half moon and died a month later, also during the period of the half moon.

"De labore solis," "from the work of the sun," referring to the solar eclipse, describes John Paul II, who has been pope since 1978. He was born on May 18, 1920, during an eclipse. The town where he was born, Vadovice, in Poland, has a sun on its coat of arms. During his pontificate, on August 11, 1999, the great solar eclipse of Europe, the last one of the millennium, occurred.

According to the prophecy the pope who follows him will be *"Gloria olivae,"* "the fame of the olive tree," and after that the prophecy warns us that "during the last persecution of the holy Roman Church, Peter II, the Roman, will reign. He will shepherd his sheep through many trials. When this is finished, the city of the seven hills will be destroyed and the terrible judge will pass judgment over his people. The end."

The end of mankind, or end of the papacy? The olive tree is the symbol of peace. Does *"gloria olivae"* stand for a short period of peace? We do not know.

An official investigation of the events of Garabandal, carried out by the Church, came to the conclusion that there were "no indications of any supernatural intervention." In fact, there was even talk of "playacting by young girls." However, two popes, Paul VI and John Paul II, spoke positively about the apparitions.

In 1992 the new bishop ordered a new examination of the existing documents and reports of eyewitnesses. He lifted all sanctions against the apparition site, but made the final recognition dependent on the occurrence of the warning and the miracle. But that, too, had been predicted. Mary had revealed to the children in 1964, "The Church will accept and recognize my having appeared to you only after the miracle."

The seers grew up to lead normal lives. Conchita married an American and moved to New York. But in the fall of 1998 she returned to Europe, and spends most of the time in Fatima now, so she can be close to Garabandal when the time for the Miracle comes. According to her this will happen soon.

CHAPTER SIXTEEN
MODERN MIRACLES

ONE OF THE most important Marian apparitions of modern times occurred on June 24, 1981, in Medjugorje, in what was then Yugoslavia, which, after a bloody war, has split up into several smaller states. Medjugorje is now in the country of Bosnia-Herzegovina.

Medjugorje is a mountain village in a region that has been plagued for centuries by religious conflicts between Catholics, members of the Orthodox church, and Muslims. These conflicts finally led to the civil war in 1991 that raged for four years before the shocked eyes of the world, putting an end to thousands of lives.

During a June afternoon ten years before the war, a mysterious globe of light was seen floating above a hill by two teenagers, sixteen-year-old Mirjana Dragiecević and her fifteen-year-old friend Ivanka

Ivanković. Within the sphere of light the girls could see the figure of a beautiful woman.

The girls returned to the hill later that evening with some other friends, and found they could still see the globe of light. This time the Lady seemed to have a child in her arms.

After they went home again, they stayed up all night and talked about what they had seen, and argued about whether it was the devil, the Mother of God, or a hallucination. The next day they returned to the hill with Vicka and Marjia, aged sixteen, and two boys, nine-year-old Jakov and sixteen-year-old Ivan. While they were climbing up the hill, a wall of light shot down from the sky that was so brilliant, they thought it was going to melt the rocks along the path.

They ran away from it, and eventually looked back to see if it was following them. To their astonishment the light had formed the shape of a cross and was moving toward the hill. When it reached the top, a woman of extraordinary beauty could be seen there. They ran back to their village to tell everyone what they'd seen.

When they returned the next day, they were followed by five thousand people, over half the village. Three flashes of lightning announced that the Virgin would be arriving soon. The teenagers started praying. Vicka turned to the crowd, some of whom hadn't believed them, and said, "Now, then, do you see we were telling the truth?"

No one apart from the children could see the

Madonna, but they all saw the brilliant light. The apparitions continued to arrive almost daily, at 6:40 P.M. Priests came to see them, along with the local Franciscan monks and the bishop.

This soon awakened the suspicion of the government of what was then Communist Yugoslavia. They feared that the apparition would stir up nationalistic ideas within the country's Catholics. The six children were summoned to appear for intensive interrogations. The parish priest, an enthusiastic supporter of the visions, was accused of subversion and sentenced to a long period of imprisonment.

Finally, it was forbidden for anyone to even go to the site of the apparitions. When that happened, pilgrims moved to the local parish church. This suited the Franciscans very well, and they incorporated the Virgin's appearances into their masses. This started a new conflict, between the Franciscans and the local clergy.

An investigative committee set up by the bishop gave a negative report on the sightings. But the Vatican came to the aid of Medjugorje. Rome gave instructions to the bishop to form a new commission to study them, which, since the apparitions are still continuing, has not yet arrived at a final judgment. The rumor is that Pope John Paul II has a positive opinion about Medjugorje. He encourages pilgrims to visit the village in the Balkans, and allegedly told Bishop Paul Hnilica in 1984, "Medjugorje is a sequel to Fatima."

Since then over twenty million pilgrims have come to

Medjugorje to witness the apparitions and hear new messages regularly, at 6:40 P.M. in the summer and 5:40 P.M. in winter. Many cures have been recorded, as well as spiritual conversions. The Mother of God promised the children, "I will give you messages such as have never been given before, since the beginning of the world." The core of her teachings is "Peace, only peace! There must be peace on earth."

These messages continued while all around Medjugorje, one of the bloodiest civil wars in European history was raging. But Medjugorje was spared, as if by a miracle. Not even one shot was fired in that mountain village and the buses bringing in pilgrims were never attacked. The site of the apparitions was an oasis of peace.

"The Holy Virgin showed me Africa and the many black people who live there," said Jelena, who has seen apparitions of the Madonna since 1982. "I saw a mother holding a child in her arms. They lived in a straw hut. They were hungry. The child was starving to death and the mother was weeping. They asked, 'Is there anyone anywhere at all who can give us a little water and a piece of bread?'

"And the Mother of God said, 'Look how they live. Is there no one who loves these people, who are your brothers and sisters?' She then showed me Asia. A war was going on. I saw men killing one another. The people were crying out in panic. Then the Mother of God showed me America. There was much luxury and many beautiful things. I saw young people sniffing drugs or injecting themselves with drugs. They thought they were happy, but the Mother of God said that they were sick if they were doing this. They, too, suffered just as much as the others I had seen."

Just like Fatima the Madonna of Medjugorje saw Russia as "the country where, in the future, God will be adored the most."

The Madonna gave Ivanka and Mirjana ten secrets, and after that she appeared to them only once a year, while the other four seers continued to see daily apparitions. According to the girls the ten secrets contain information, with definite dates, about the last chapter of the history of the world and the punishments that will come to mankind. The Madonna has assured them that all these events will take place during their lives. After the secrets have been fulfilled, the Madonna will not appear on earth again.

Ten days before each of the events is predicted to occur, Mirjana is to reveal the relevant secret to Father Ljubičič, whose job it is to inform the world. The first secret, the girls say, will destroy the power of Satan over the world. The third secret will be a permanent, indestructible sign on the hill at Medjugorje where the vision occurred for the first time. The same sign will appear at Garabandal as well. Following that there will be a short period of grace and conversion. After the tenth secret is fulfilled, "those left on earth will live in harmony with God," which may hint that mankind will be returned to a primitive state, just as Einstein predicted.

The children describe the vision this way: "We see her as one sees a person. She has black, slightly curly hair and blue eyes."

"She is slim, beautiful, and transparent," says another. "I'd love to just keep on looking at her, she is so beautiful. She wears a white veil and a dress below that. The tone of her voice cannot be described, it's as if she were singing. A light announces her coming at first, by flashing three times and then once more."

A series of scientific investigations have confirmed that the apparitions at Medjugorje are genuine. The first was a psychological examination of the seer children that was carried out as early as June 1981 by order of the authorities. Two female doctors from nearby psychiatric clinics were convinced that the children were absolutely normal. They said to them, "If anyone is mad at all, it is the ones who sent you here. There is nothing wrong with you at all."

Again, in 1982 and 1983, the psychiatrist Dr. Ludwik Stopar examined the children and came to the same decision. Neurological exams showed that they did not exhibit any pathological symptoms. Italian doctors who conducted similar tests confirmed this evaluation.

They all paid particular attention to the condition of ecstasy among the teenagers, which shows the same characteristics as that of the children at Garabandal. Initially, the seers all drop down on their knees simultaneously. It is as if their voices are switched off, for their lips move silently. Their voices become audible again only when they begin to say the Lord's Prayer. At the end of the vision all of them simultaneously raise their heads and eyes upward, as they follow the disappearing apparition.

Nothing scientific can explain how they are all able to suddenly kneel down at once. They give no sideways glances and make no gestures to signal one another. Instead they all look in the same direction of the cross and kneel down together, as if they were impelled to do so by a single force. Clinical examinations rule out hallucinatory phenomena as well as epilepsy, and there are no signs of any hypnotic suggestion.

Dr. Maria Frederica Magatti investigated the depth of their ecstatic state by calling the children, touching and pushing them, even by sticking needles into their bodies, but the children did not show any reaction whatsoever. When the light from a thousand-watt projector was beamed directly into their eyes, they showed no reaction. Their pupils did not change in size and they didn't even blink.

During the summer of 1984 Professor Joyeux, neurologist of the University of Montpelier in France, together with his team of experts, conducted a series of tests for which, before and during the apparitions, the children were connected to electroencephalogram machines, which measured their brain waves. The results showed the children were "in the alpha rhythm. This is the rhythm of wakefulness and receptivity, of calm contemplation. Before the apparitions the seers are in the beta rhythm, but as soon as the ecstasy sets in, they drop down to the alpha rhythm."

This EEG result, says Professor Joyeux, "excludes epilepsy." In addition, eye tests revealed that at the beginning of the apparitions the natural movements of the eyeballs stopped. Eye movements that are associated with attention to the outside world begin again at the end of the apparitions, in each child at the exact same time. During the apparitions the eyes did not react in any way to external stimuli.

There were occasions when the alternate reality of the visions broke through into the concrete world and were observed by thousands of people. A cross has been set up at the site, on top of the hill, and it has often been noticed that it glows as if it was made of neon.

On August 2, 1981, about 150 witnesses saw a "dance of the sun," like the one at Fatima. The sun begun to rotate on its axis, shot down toward the people, and then retreated. Other solar miracles were seen in 1984.

The authorities cordoned off the hill for a time. In October 1981 all the people in the village observed a fire burning on the hill where the visions had taken place. The fire burned all through the night. The next day, although the hill was still out of bounds, one of the villagers managed to get to the place where the fire had been seen, but found no signs of it. That was the prelude to a great sign. "All these signs are given to you to strengthen your faith until I send the permanent sign," said the Mother of God to the children the next day.

On December 19, 1981, the local newspaper announced, "During the last days a white light has been observed above the hill. A white figure was seen under the cross, and then the cross became white. Today at 11:30 A.M. the cross changed into a thin white column, then took on the apparition of the slim figure of the Mother of God, like a silhouette. A number of people in various places saw this."

In 1984 two witnesses, Piero Sestini of Florence and Louis Desrippes from Bordeaux, were filming the hill, when the cross mysteriously disappeared and then reappeared again. In Desrippes's film the cross changed into a great ball on which could be seen the silhouette of a woman. On June 25, 1984, a group of pilgrims saw a star appearing and disappearing above the hill of the cross.

Even today apparitions still occur in Medjugorje, and messages are regularly transmitted to the pilgrims who come there. Mysterious phenomena are observed. Anyone who is seriously looking for an opportunity to witness a Marian apparition, with all its related phenomena, will find it at Medjugorje. It's a miracle that is happening today, in the modern world.

Still, visitors should remember that Medjugorje is still highly controversial and far from being officially acknowledged by the Church. Its critics point to the growing commercialization of the events and the growing banality of the messages. The last word on Medjugorje is far from being spoken. Since 1981 over twenty million pilgrims have visited the place, and over 330 cases of healing have been reported.

The Madonna appeared again, just before a time of civil war, in Rwanda on November 28, 1981. Seven teenagers saw apparitions of the Madonna and Her Son, during which she predicted the slaughter that devastated the country during the mid 1990s. Three of the seers were pupils at a school run by nuns at Kibeho, the other four lived in the bush. Their ages varied from thirteen to twenty-three. Vestine, the oldest, was a Muslim. Sagatashya, whose parents followed their tribal religion, had never even heard the name of Jesus before.

Jesus and Mary appeared to the seven children individually during their daily activities. When the twenty-two-year-old Agnes, a girl from a Catholic family, had her vision, other witnesses saw the sun rotating.

Vestine, the Muslim girl, fell into a trance that lasted from Good Friday to Easter Monday in 1983. She said later that during this period she traveled to a different place, outside the earth, in the company of the Mother of God. She visited a huge universe, different from ours. This is the same sort of thing that is described over and over again, by people who claim to have been abducted by aliens.

During her apparition on August 19, 1982, the Mother of God shed tears and the children wept with her. She then showed them in a vision the future of Rwanda. They saw a river of blood that flowed through the streets, which were lined by mutilated corpses.

People were fighting everywhere, and hell seemed to have broken loose. On August 15, 1988, the apparitions were acknowledged as genuine by the Catholic bishop of Rwanda, and a stream of pilgrims started coming there. One of the seer children declared, "The world is coming to an end." For many of the children of that country the world they knew was to end very soon.

The worship of the Madonna was interrupted when the civil war broke out. The Hutu and Tutsi tribes carried out one of the worst massacres in history. Of the 8.2 million inhabitants of Rwanda, 1 million were slaughtered, and 2.4 million fled the country. One hundred fifty thousand people died in epidemics in the refugee camps. Over a hundred clergymen, among them the bishop of Kigali, were killed, and dozens of churches destroyed. At least three of the seers lost their lives during the killings, and the fate of two more is uncertain, while two of them managed to reach a refugee camp.

The examples of the apparitions of Rwanda and Medjugorje show us the seriousness of the warnings received through Marian apparitions. Perhaps these catastrophes could have been prevented, if Mary's advice had been taken seriously.

I have pointed out some similarities between Marian visions and UFO sightings. On April 23, 1994, in Brazil, a UFO organization finally managed to investigate an apparition.

José Ernani, a pious young man twenty-five years old, was praying, when suddenly a luminous figure stood in front of him. She announced that she would return on the first days of September and October in 1994.

Over three thousand believers arrived on September 1, to be present when the Holy Virgin appeared again as she had promised. Witnesses confirm that when she returned, shortly after 2:30 P.M., the sun darkened and looked like the full moon.

Their reports convinced scientists at the Brazilian UFO Research Center to come to the next apparition. While over five thousand believers prayed, they waited with their static-electricity detectors, magnetic-field detectors, and photographic and video cameras ready. Shortly before 2:00 P.M. José Ernani returned and knelt in prayer to receive his vision.

"Suddenly clouds came together in the sky as if they were moved by an unseen hand," one of the scientists, Reginaldo de Athayde, reported. "They formed a big, dark cloud that covered the sun. The cloud then stopped moving, although the other clouds still moved at normal speed. We felt a comfortable breeze, loaded with static electricity, which gave us goose bumps on our skin. The breeze blew as if it wanted to refresh the tired, sweating believers. They all prayed, and some cried hysterically and asked the Virgin for forgiveness for their sins.

"The people were falling on their knees, their eyes directed to the sky. The cloud hovered over the ground, with the sun shining behind it in multicolored rays. A silver circle, as large as the moon, formed and disappeared. Cries and tears, prayers and religious songs, could be heard. The seer, who was in a trancelike ecstasy, repeated the message that was given to him by the Mother of God. At 2:05 everything went back to normal.

"But then something else happened. Up in the sky a silver object as big as the moon was visible next to the sun. Then it disappeared again. The sky returned to normal and only the usual clouds could be seen.

"Suddenly someone pointed to the sky, shouting, 'Look at the pearls of the rosary of the Virgin.' Our researchers Paulo Cesar Tavora and Helio Loyola directed their cameras toward the spheres, which were three in a row, clearly visible, disk-shaped and metallic.

"The electronic engineer, Dr. Tavora, was responsible for the measurement instruments. He told us that he detected electromagnetic fields of ten impulses per second when the seer spoke with the Madonna, confirming the presence of strong static electricity. He was surprised that the electricity pulsed, instead of steadily increasing. He had no explanation for this phenomenon."

Is this evidence that Marian apparitions are really UFO visitations? Or is this scientific confirmation of a modern miracle?

CHAPTER SEVENTEEN
WHY AND HOW

THE APPARITIONS OF the Virgin Mary don't happen only abroad; they happen near your hometown as well, right here in the United States. They became a reality for Joseph Januszkiewicz of Marlboro Township, New Jersey, in the late 1980s. The fifty-six-year-old Polish immigrant went into the garden to pray in front of a blue-eyed statue of the Madonna, which he had brought back from a trip abroad and installed there. Suddenly the real Mother of God appeared, floating over a group of trees.

Januszkiewicz called his wife, who sprayed holy water around, fearing that it could be a demonic trick. The vision reacted with a gentle smile, and promised to come back. Since then she has returned at regular intervals.

Since 1992 she has called herself "the Yellow Rose of

Peace" and has instructed Joseph to report his experiences. She promised to appear on the first Sunday of every month, at dusk. Crowds of people have come to see her, up to ten thousand a day. Even police blockades couldn't stop them. Many of them left their cars and walked for miles to get to the Januszkiewicz site.

Some people in Lake Ridge, Virginia, had another type of Marian experience. Many of them work for the CIA, the FBI, the Pentagon, or other government agencies. They drive expensive cars and carry cell phones, and Catholics there practice a modern type of Christianity, without any mysticism. Then, in December 1991, the priest of the Saint Elizabeth Ann Seton Church, Father James Bruse, began to bleed from his hands and feet, and this changed their lives.

At first the priest hid his stigmata. He consulted a psychiatrist and a specialist in internal medicine, who both told him he was in normal physical and psychological condition. But then, in March 1992, the gold-painted fiberglass Madonna of his church started to weep in front of five hundred people, and he confessed his secret.

Since then pilgrims have brought their statues of the Madonna to the church, and many of these have also started to weep tears. Other people claim to have been healed, and others say they have seen a solar miracle.

Signs and miracles are reported all over the United States. Theresa Lopez claims to have seen the Madonna on the second Sunday of every month since 1991, from Lookout Mountain in Colorado. In Conyers, Georgia, housewife Nancy Fowler has been hooked up to an EEG recorder during her monthly conversations with the Virgin. The results of the tests revealed that "when Mary comes there are changes in the concentration of energies," neuropsychologist Dr. Ricardo Castanon explained. "We can register exactly the times when Mary is speaking."

A picture depicting the Heart of Jesus that belongs to a member of the San José parish of Austin, Texas, began to bleed on January 11, 1991, when the Gulf War started. When the seer noticed it, he called his family, and discovered that two members of the family had had visions of a war. The family brought the picture to the church, where it was exhibited to the public. The image continued to bleed, and many believers were healed and received messages.

Toward the end of July a member of the community received a message from Mary, announcing her appearance on August 15. She asked them to say the rosary between 1:00 and 3:00 P.M., and promised "something very beautiful in the sky." During the prayer many witnesses had visions of the Virgin, and others were healed.

After the prayer about five or six hundred believers waited to see the miracle. At 4:15 P.M. the sun began to rotate. People saw this sign in the heavens without any discomfort to their eyes. Since then the Heart of Jesus picture stands in a small wooden shrine. A stone building is being built for it. The priest of the community, Fred Underwood, said, "I have never experienced the Lord acting so powerfully. We have had dozens of healings and conversions. The Lord is speaking to the people."

A cleaning woman was the first to discover a weeping statue of the Virgin Mary in the Church of Our Lady of Guadalupe in San Antonio, Texas. The pastor, Tony Ozzimo, was "astounded and surprised" by the miracle, and thousands poured into the church, situated in the poor, Mexican side of the town. A six-year-old paralyzed girl was healed when she was told by the Madonna to get up and walk.

An hour's drive from Los Angeles several miracles occurred in a suburban neighborhood. Crosses of light and crosses of shadow appeared, a picture of the Virgin emerged on the glass of a window, and finally, a statue of Mary, belonging to a woman from Kuwait, produced tears of oil. Tests revealed that the oil was five hundred years old.

Eventually, in January 1991, the statue of María poured out tears of blood and said, "I am weeping on account of the war," meaning the Gulf War. "I want you to pray the rosary every day at three P.M." There followed further apparitions and messages, including some secrets for the Vatican, which the priest of the community brought to Rome personally.

What does this all mean? Why is a worldwide increase in miracles occurring at this time? Could it be hysteria, similar to that of the first millennium, when Christians expected the end of the world, and thousands of despairing people gave away all their possessions and ran through the streets, whipping themselves until they bled?

But some of these miracles can be photographed, or, as in the case of the weeping Madonnas, they have signs that can be studied scientifically. Everything indicates that someone from another level of existence is trying to get in contact with us, and wants to tell us something. Ten years of extraordinary crop circles in England and other parts of the world show us this as well. Is mankind standing on the verge of self-destruction? Many UFO visitors have given warnings about ecological breakdown.

Naturally, the first question is whether the things that happened at Fatima were really supernatural. The Fatima predictions can be seen as genuine for the following reasons: First, the messages given went far beyond the children's knowledge and comprehension. The fact that almost the entire twentieth century, from 1917 to 1991, would be characterized by the conflict with Communism, would have been impossible to imagine in 1917, and certainly not by three little Portuguese shepherd children. Also, the Madonna correctly predicted the beginning of the Second World War, with the bloodred aurora borealis as its herald.

The Fatima phenomena were seen by skeptics, as well as believers, ruling out mass hysteria. The "miracle of the sun" was visible in neighboring villages as well as in Fatima. And the visions of August 13, 1917, occurred when the children were away from the site, in custody at Ourém.

There is an almost uncanny connection between the Fatima events and the course of history during the twentieth century. The decisive turning points of World War II, and Gorbachev's "perestroika," followed immediately after the consecration of the world and Russia to the Immaculate Heart, as demanded in the visions.

The new science of quantum physics has discovered that an implicit order pervades the cosmos—in other words, everything is connected with everything else. According to German physicist Max Planck, "We may say that, according to everything science teaches us, there is an order which is independent of humanity, but one which can be described as acting with a purpose. It represents a sensible universal order, by which nature and humanity are governed, but its true character remains unknown to us." He postulated the existence of an "almighty intelligence that rules over Nature." This sounds like a scientist who has discovered God.

Or, as the NASA physicist Robert Jastrow has said, "The scientist has climbed the mountains of ignorance painstakingly and diligently. He is about to reach the peak, but when he drags himself across the last ridge, he is greeted there by a group of mystics and religious leaders, who have been waiting for him for thousands of years."

The "holographic view of the universe," as the British scientist Ken Wilber calls it, has been proposed by Planck, Einstein, and many other major scientists. Cambridge biochemist Rupert Sheldrake says that the entire universe is a hologram, and each individual element reflects the totality. Thus the human brain represents a complete picture of the world, and can receive the information of the entire macrocosmos.

The psychologists Anderson and Bentov originated the thesis that the entire information of the universe is encoded holographically in the energy pattern that constantly bombards us. "Meditation," they say (and prayer, I must add), "can quiet the brain to such an extent that it is in tune with the universal frequency pattern. If this happens, the coded information regarding the universe is decoded and the individual experiences a state of being one with the universe."

This is confirmed by the EEG tests done on the modern seers. These tests showed that in deep meditation, the cerebral cortex becomes synchronized with the apparition. The most successful meditation practices, in the opinion of these psychologists, come from Hindu and Buddhist traditions, as the constant repetition of a certain word or phrase. A repetitive prayer like the rosary can work the same way.

Through repeated prayers and chanting, "alpha rhythm" brain-wave frequencies can be achieved, which form the state of greatest relaxation and receptivity. This type of brain-wave pattern was noted in the children of Medjugorje, during their states of religious ecstasy. Is a human being in this state able to receive messages from an ultimate power?

Another frequent demand, expressed by most Marian

apparitions, is that a chapel be built where people can pray to her for peace. It's doubtful that the Mother of God needs to beg for adoration, so what is going on here?

Scientific experiments conducted with large groups of people who are meditating have shown that people in the alpha level can collectively build up strong fields of consciousness. Dr. Rupert Sheldrake talks about "morphogenetic fields," an expression he invented. Sheldrake is convinced that these fields exist in and around every organism, just as a magnetic field exists around a magnet. He says, "The morphogenetic fields of all organisms are all connected to one another by morphic resonance. This morphic resonance is the guiding power beyond the material world. It binds everything together and determines the course of evolution."

Hundreds of experiments made all over the world seem to confirm Sheldrake's hypothesis. They all lead to one result: the greater the number of people who learn something, the quicker it's learned by people who study it afterward. The greater the number of people who accept a certain idea, the faster the idea spreads.

The biologist Lyall Watson had already discovered this effect in 1952, which he called the "hundredth monkey" theory. He was studying the habits of a colony of monkeys on the isolated Japanese island of Koshima. The animals lived mainly on sweet potatoes, which were supplied to them in an unwashed state by the scientists involved in the project. One time a female monkey discovered that the potatoes tasted better if she washed them in the water before eating them. The younger monkeys copied this and soon all of them were washing their food before eating it.

"That was the beginning of a cultural revolution," said Watson. To prove his thesis Watson counted the number of monkeys who washed their potatoes. At 11:00 A.M. he counted ninety-nine, so when soon another one did it, it became the "hundredth monkey." But then a quantum leap occurred; on the evening of the same day all the monkeys on the island, without exception, were washing their potatoes in water. But not only these—the monkeys on other islands and also on the mainland followed this practice, without having any contact with the monkeys of the island.

It's clear that a sufficiently large number of intelligent minds, working in tandem, can program a consciousness field, which can then alter the behavior of others or cause the explosive spread of an idea. Does this mean that if a sufficient number of people pray for peace, the idea of peace will spread throughout the world? It is certainly an experiment worth trying.

Perhaps places of pilgrimage serve as places where "a hundred monkeys" can unite to produce a field of consciousness that can change the present, or the future. A classic example of this law at work is the consecration of Russia to the Immaculate Heart of Mary. Pope Pius XII did his best to fulfill the wish of the Madonna, but did not achieve the desired effect. Why not? This consecration was supposed to have been performed publicly, in order to build up a worldwide field of consciousness through millions of praying people, who would simultaneously concentrate on one thought—their desire for the conversion of Russia.

This was not to be merely a sentimental and antiquated ceremony, but a practical act, to reprogram the human morphogenetic field and aim it toward peace. When Pope John Paul II finally performed the ceremony as recommended, the effect was felt within a year. "But the consecration was done too late, far too late," declared Lúcia. Moreover, the consecration wasn't specific enough, and was only halfhearted. Instead of a new, holy Russia, we see today a shaky country, torn by internal crises.

The many Marian visions that are occurring all over the world are something we should take seriously. No matter how terrible the future may be, it can only be altered by the knowledge, hopes, and prayers of millions and millions of us, from all religions, throughout the world. If we can learn to think and meditate together, we can change the future of mankind.

The great number of warnings we have received in recent times indicates how great the dangers are that threaten us. But they also let us know that we are not alone.

CHAPTER EIGHTEEN
REVELATION

I write in obedience to you, my God, who commanded me to do so through his Excellency the Bishop of Leiria and through your Most Holy Mother and mine.

After the two parts which I have already explained, at the left of Our Lady and a little above, we saw an angel with a flaming sword in his left hand. Flashing, it gave out flames that looked as though they would set the world on fire, but they died out in contact with the splendor that Our Lady radiated toward him from her right hand.

Pointing to the earth with his right hand, the angel cried out in a loud voice: "Penance, Penance, Penance!"

And we saw in an immense light that is God

something similar to how people appear in a mirror when they pass in front of it—a bishop dressed in white. We had the impression that it was the Holy Father.

Other bishops, priests, religious men and women, were going up a steep mountain, at the top of which there was a big cross of rough-hewn trunks as of a cork tree with the bark [on it].

Before reaching there, the Holy Father passed through a big city half in ruins. Half-trembling, with halting steps, afflicted with pain and sorrow, he prayed for the souls of the corpses he met on his way.

Having reached the top of the mountain, on his knees at the foot of the big cross, he was killed by a group of soldiers who fired bullets and arrows at him.

In the same way, there died, one after another, the bishops, priests, religious men and women, and various laypeople of different ranks and positions.

Beneath the two arms of the cross, there were two angels, each with a crystal aspersorium [a vessel for holding holy water] in his hand, in which they gathered up the blood of the martyrs and with it sprinkled the souls that were making their way to God.

The text of the Third Secret of Fatima, as written down by Lúcia dos Santos on March 1st, 1944.

Fatima, Portugal, May 12, 2000. The streets leading to the Portuguese sanctuary were crowded as never before.

Over 600,000 people were there to witness a historic event. The pope was coming to Fatima for the third time; this time the official reason for his journey was the beatification of two of the three little shepherds, Francisco and Jacinta, who died in 1919 and 1920.

The documentation of a miracle at Fatima by the Vatican Congregation for the Cause of the Saints had finally put Francisco and Jacinta on the road to sainthood. That happened when a sixty-nine-year-old Portuguese woman, Maria Emilia Santos, who had lain in bed paralyzed for twenty-two years, found she could walk again after she prayed to the two children. The case was investigated by a medical commission headed by Professor Raffaello Cortesini. The physicians found no scientific explanation for the sudden healing, so for the Church, it was a sign from the heavens. In December 1998, the complete documentation of the case was presented to the pope, who immediately, on December 19, gave his "nihil obstat," or permission.

On April 16, 1999, Monsignor Paolo Molinari, the postulator of the congregation, publicly announced the upcoming beatification, without revealing any details about when and where it would occur. In most cases, beatifications take place in Rome at St. Peter's Square, especially during a Holy Year packed with official observances by the Holy Father. But the pope decided to go to Fatima instead. When the Portuguese bishops visited Rome in November 1999, the pope said good-bye to them with the words "Arrivederci a Fatima"—"See you in Fatima"—at least that's what Serafim da Silva, bishop of Leiria and Fatima, told the press on November 26, 1999. Officially, the Vatican kept silent. The health of the ailing pontiff did not seem stable enough for him to promise to make such an arduous journey. Only after he completed his historic pilgrimage to the Holy Land in March 2000 was it announced that he would return to Fatima.

The pope wanted the trip to be a special event, a highlight of the Vatican's Jubilee Year, a yearlong celebration of two thousand years of Christianity. He wanted to pray to the Holy Virgin at the actual apparition site, to ask her to protect Christianity in the third millennium. And, since it was only five days before his eightieth birthday, he wanted to thank her for granting him nineteen more years of life, as he is convinced she saved his life during the assassination attempt of 1981.

Would he also finally reveal the contents of the Third Secret? Rumors circulated; nothing was certain. "The pope is always good for a surprise," was the cryptic comment made by Cardinal Joseph Ratzinger only a few days before the trip. He had opposed publication of the Secret in the past, fearing sensationalism.

A week before the trip, on May 7, 2000, John Paul II held an extraordinary and moving ceremony in the Roman Coliseum, where he honored what he called the "new martyrs," including members of the Protestant and Orthodox churches. "The courage they demonstrated in taking up the Cross of Christ calls out to us with a voice louder than any factors of division," the pope explained.

The names of 12,692 martyrs of the twentieth century were read out at this ceremony—first, the victims of Soviet Communism and Nazism, but also those from the Spanish and Mexican revolutions in the twenties and thirties and, more recently, from the People's Republic of China, Indonesia, and Africa. Altogether more Christians died for their faith in the last century than during the two-and-a-half centuries of the Roman Empire.

It was raining heavily when finally, after three hours had passed and darkness had fallen in Rome, John Paul II said a final prayer. Preparing this extensive list of the victims of religious persecution—both priests and laymen—had been one of the most important projects the Holy Father requested for the Jubilee. Did he want to prove that the Fatima prophecy, to be revealed the following week, was correct?

Expectations were high when the pope arrived in the sanctuary on the evening of May 12. He was obviously exhausted as he stepped out of the military helicopter that brought him from Lisbon to Fatima. At the Lisbon airport, he met the Portuguese president Jorge Sampaio. About a hundred children, some from the same hospital where Jacinta had died eighty years ago, greeted him, waving flags in the Vatican colors of white and yellow.

In Fatima, a crowd gathered near the sanctuary and enthusiastically welcomed the pontiff, who greeted them from his bullet-proof white Popemobile. Half a million people, cheering and waving white handkerchiefs, noticed how tired he seemed as he climbed out of his vehicle and slowly mounted the few steps up to the Capelinha, the little chapel built at the request of the Madonna. A statue stands in front of it, which was carved according to the descriptions of the three shepherd children.

There was profound silence as the pope knelt and spent several minutes in deep prayer before he presented a very special gift to the chapel, the ring given to him by his teacher, the late Polish cardinal Stefan Wyszynski, after he was elected pope in 1978. "You will lead the Church into the third millennium," the Polish cardinal had predicted. This ring was the most precious gift John Paul II could offer. With this act, he dedicated his entire pontificate to Our Lady of Fatima, and demonstrated the importance of the Fatima apparitions. It may have been a farewell gift as well, since it does not seem likely he will live long enough to return to the shrine.

After blessing the crowd, the pope left the sanctuary again. The solemn mass, followed by a procession of lights, took place without him. He had to rest up in preparation for the following day.

I stood in the crowd and watched the mass that day. I had come to Fatima to participate in an event that I felt would be remembered in history. I got up early the next morning to join the streams of people flowing to the shrine in the early hours of May 13, 2000. Ten thousand people were already at the sanctuary square when I arrived, having spent the chilly night in sleeping bags, in their cars, in tents and campers. We were all greeted by a warming sun which, together with a steel-blue sky, promised a beautiful spring day. Over 600,000 people were squeezed into the rotunda when, precisely at 8:30 A.M., the Holy Father entered the sanctuary in his Popemobile.

An hour earlier, before he arrived for the beatification ceremony, he'd had an important date in the sacristy of the Basilica of Fatima. There he met the third shepherd seer, Sister Lúcia, now ninety-three years old, who had made one of her rare trips outside her convent, the Carmel of Coimbra, exclusively for this event. It might be the last time she ever saw the site of the apparitions, or talked personally with the pope.

Later it was revealed that they discussed details of an upcoming revelation of the Third Secret. On October 8, 2000, when hundreds of bishops from all over the world would arrive in Rome for the Jubilee of the Bishops, the Holy Father wanted to renew the consecration of the world and Russia to Our Lady of Fatima. He hoped to be invited to visit Russia in 2001. He was hoping to witness the fulfillment of the promise of the Virgin when she said, "The Holy Father will consecrate Russia to me, she will convert, and a time of peace will come."

The statue of Our Lady was carried in a procession to the front of the basilica; then the pope, followed by Sister Lúcia, entered and was greeted by the enthusiastic crowd. Next came the ceremony of the beatification of Francisco and Jacinta, whose pictures were displayed on both sides of the tower of the basilica. Eventually, John Paul II referred to his personal involvement in the Fatima events: "And once again I would like to celebrate the Lord's goodness to me when I was saved from death after being gravely wounded on May 13, 1981."

Not until the end of the two-and-a-half hour ceremony, during which Sister Lúcia received the Holy Communion from the hands of the pope, was the Secret revealed. After the hundreds of priests who had walked out into the crowd to distribute the blessed sacrament returned to their places, a speech by Cardinal Sodano, the secretary of state for the Vatican, was announced.

"Brothers and sisters in the Lord," he said in Portuguese, "on this solemn occasion of his visit to Fatima, His Holiness has directed me to make an announcement to you. As you know, the purpose of his visit to Fatima has been to beatify the two little shepherds. Nevertheless, he also wants his pilgrimage here to be seen as a renewed gesture of gratitude to Our Lady for her protection during these years of his papacy. This protection seems to also be linked to the third part of the Secret of Fatima. . . . The Pope has asked the Congregation for the Doctrine of the Faith to reveal the third part of the Secret, after they prepare an appropriate commentary. . . ."

As he said these words, a murmur went through the crowd. Those who were close to the altar were able to observe the reaction of the Holy Father and Sister Lúcia. They saw a look of satisfaction on the face of the pope.

Lúcia seemed as happy as a child, untouched by the burden of her ninety-three years, although she needed a cane and another nun's help to get up from her knees after the mass. Now that her mission was finally fulfilled, she could spend the last years of her life in peace.

"The vision of Fatima concerns, above all, the war waged by atheistic systems against the Church and Christians, and it describes the immense sufferings endured by the witnesses of the faith in the last century of the second millennium," Cardinal Sodano continued.

"According to the interpretation of the little shepherds, which was also confirmed recently by Sister Lúcia, 'the Bishop clothed in white' who prays for all the faithful is the pope. As he makes his way with great difficulty towards the cross amid the corpses of those who were martyred (bishops, priests, religious men and women, and many laypeople), he too falls to the ground, apparently dead, under a hail of gunfire."

The moment he said this, it was as if I—and the crowd of 600,000 around me—were all struck by lightning. In 1917, did the Holy Virgin really predict the assassination attempt on the pope with this degree of precision? There could be no better description of the events of May 13, 1981. Now it was apparent that this event was a milestone in the millennium scenario of the Madonna.

When John Paul II read the contents of the Third Secret after the assassination attempt, the plan of divine providence became clear to him. Everything in his life

suddenly took on new meaning. The fact that he came
from Poland, and had personally experienced the terror
of Nazism and the suffering of Christians under
Communism, must have made the words about the consecration of Russia especially meaningful to him. And finally, the assassination attempt—all this was part of a
great plan in which he, as an instrument of God, had to
play his role.

From that moment on, the pope tried to follow the requests of the Madonna in everything he did. When the
bishop of Leiria and Fatima visited Rome, John Paul gave
him the bullet which was found in his Jeep after the shots
were fired on St. Peter's square. It was inserted into the
crown of the miraculous image of Our Lady of Fatima in
order to bear witness that it was indeed Her hand that
guided the bullet's path, enabling the pope to halt at the
threshold of death. When the walls of Eastern Europe
crumbled in 1989, and when the Soviet era ended on
December 31, 1991, he knew that she had kept her promise. Now he could concentrate on his second great goal, to
lead mankind into the third millennium, for which the
Mother of God had promised an "era of peace."

On June 26, 2000, the promise given by Cardinal
Sodano that the Third Secret would be published, as ordered by Pope John Paul II, was fulfilled. The Holy See
announced a press conference for 11:30 A.M. that day,
during which the document of the message of Fatima
would be presented. Journalists and TV teams from all
over the world crowded in front of the Sala Stampa on

Rome's Via della Conciliazione hours ahead of time. A live radio broadcast to forty countries was prepared. "No explanation was ever expected with so much tension," the Italian daily newspaper *Corriere della Sera* printed the night before. "Only the election of the pope caused more anticipation."

In February 2000, Pope John Paul II had informed the prefect of the Congregation for the Doctrine of the Faith, Cardinal Joseph Ratzinger, about his plan to release the Third Secret, together with a commentary. On April 19, 2000, he dictated a letter to "the Reverend Sister Maria Lúcia" in which he asked her to speak with the secretary of the congregation, Archbishop Tarcisio Bertone, and answer all his questions.

On April 27, Monsignor Bertone, together with the bishop of Leiria and Fatima, Serafim de Sousa Ferreir a Silva, arrived at the Carmel convent in Coimbra. In what the archbishop described as a relaxed and cheerful atmosphere, Lúcia agreed to cooperate as much as possible. She "was lucid and at ease; she was very happy that the Holy Father was going to Fatima," he said.

Monsignor Bertone showed her the envelope with the Third Secret inside, which he had brought with him from Rome. After touching it with her fingers, she immediately stated, "This is my letter," and then, while reading it, said, "This is my writing."

Archbishop Bertone said, "Sister Lúcia agreed with the interpretation that the third part of the secret was a prophetic vision, similar to those in religious history. She repeated her conviction that the vision of Fatima concerns above all the struggle of atheist Communism against the Church and against Christians, and describes the terrible sufferings of the victims of the faith in the twentieth century."

"Is the principal figure in the vision the pope?" Bertone asked. Lúcia at once replied that it was. "We did not know the name of the pope. Our Lady did not tell us his name, so we did not know whether it was Benedict XV or Pius XII or Paul VI or John Paul II, but it was the pope who was suffering and that made us suffer, too."

Some important events occurred before the Secret was revealed. On Monday, June 5, 2000, the newly elected Russian president Vladimir Putin visited the Vatican for a confidential meeting. Later it was rumored that the visit was disappointing for the pope. He had hoped the Russian president would bring him an invitation to visit Moscow.

A visit by John Paul II to Russia is heavily opposed by the Russian Orthodox Patriarch Alexej II, who fears the intrusion of Roman Catholicism into his country. But the Pope has still not given up hope that eventually this dream too will be fulfilled, with the help of Our Lady of Fatima.

On June 14, 2000, the would-be assassin Ali Agca was pardoned by Italy's president, Carlo Azeglio Campi. This was discussed with the Vatican beforehand and supported by the pope. The forty-three-year-old Turk was immediately returned to his country and placed in a high security prison in Istanbul, where he is now serving ten years for murder of the editor-in-chief of the newspaper *Milliyet.*

In several interviews with the Italian press, he described himself as "an ignorant instrument in a mysterious plan." The announcement of Cardinal Sodano, he claimed, was for him "the last piece of the puzzle, which helped me to understand that both of us, myself and the pope, were merely playing our roles in a drama written by God, eternal and Almighty."

The Roman daily newspaper *La Repubblica* wrote of the pope, ". . . his brush with death gave his long duel with the Communist system a special greatness. What the pope represented did not fall, but the Soviet colossus and the Berlin wall did."

After the revelation of the Third Secret, Cardinal Ratzinger tried his best to explain that the horrific Fatima vision of the pope climbing over corpses in the midst of a ruined city should not be taken literally. First of all, he stated, it was a private revelation. There is no obligation for a Christian to believe in it. Still, private revelations can help us to understand the signs of the time.

"In every age," he said, "the Church has received prophecies, which must be scrutinized but not scorned." Yet the Fatima message was more than that. Never before did the Church care so much about keeping a revelation secret, and never before was one finally revealed with so much care. The Third Secret was the key prophecy for the Church in the twentieth century.

Prophecy does not need to be an accurate prediction of the future. Ratzinger said, "In this case, prediction of the future is of secondary importance. What is essential is the reality of the definite revelation." The best biblical example for the role of prophecy is the book of Jonah. "And the word of the Lord reached Jonah, saying, 'Arise and go to Nineveh, that great city, and declare my word . . . Only forty days and Nineveh will perish!' " (Chapters I:1–2 and III:4) Nineveh was the capital of the Assyrian empire, the Washington, D.C. of its time. But when the Ninevites listened to the prophet, they recognized that they were on a wrong path and corrected it— and Nineveh was saved.

When a prophecy is listened to, and an appropriate reaction follows, it seems as if the predicted events do not have to occur. This may be one way to interpret the prophecies of Fatima—as a warning, not a prediction of the future.

How does a vision like Fatima happen? The soul of the seer, Cardinal Ratzinger explained, "is touched by something real, even if it is beyond the senses. He is then able to know things which cannot be seen. The person is led beyond the exterior of life and is touched by deeper dimensions of reality, which then become visible to him." He explained why simple shepherd children were the ones who received these visions. "Their souls were not yet given over to the world, their interior powers of perception were still not impaired."

But just as life reaches us through the filter of our

senses, the seer must also translate his vision, in order to understand it. Cardinal Ratzinger explained that, "The subject shares in the formation of the image he sees. He can arrive at the image only within the bounds of his capacities and possibilities. Such visions therefore are never simple photographs of another world, but are influenced by the limitations of the person who sees them. For this reason, the language of visions is symbolic."

As Sister Lúcia wrote to Pope John Paul II in the letter she handed to him on his first visit to Fatima on May 12, 1982, "The third part of the secret is a symbolic revelation, based on whether or not we accept what the message itself asks of us."

We can assume that she refers to the words in the second part of the Fatima Secret that state, "If not, [Russia] will spread her errors throughout the world, causing wars and persecutions of the Church. The good will be martyred, the Holy Father will have much to suffer, various nations will be annihilated." The image of a world reduced to rubble and strewn with corpses, where the faithful are killed, is symbolic of a world fallen to Communism.

Whether or not that vision came true depended upon whether the Church was willing to consecrate Russia to Mary, according to the dictates of the Lady of Fatima. As we know, the Church hesitated to do this out of fear of Russia's power, but John Paul II finally obeyed her command, at first in secret, then openly, and mighty Russia fell.

Cardinal Ratzinger claimed that the angel with the flaming sword "represents the threat of judgment which looms over the world. Today the possibility that the world could be reduced to ashes by a sea of fire no longer seems like pure fantasy; man himself, with his inventions, has forged the flaming sword." But the Mother of God was against this, and instead the angel called loudly for penance. "In this way, the importance of human freedom is emphasized." We have the choice between self-destruction and a return to God. We must completely discount all fatalistic interpretations of the Secret—our future is in human hands.

Ratzinger stated that the destroyed city, the mountain, and the cross all represent the "arena of human history," with the cross (standing for faith) as its goal. The bishops, priests and religious people represent the church. "In the vision we can recognize the last century as a century of martyrs, a century of suffering and persecution for the Church, a century of world wars and many local wars."

In its center is the figure of the pope, and there is danger that he too might fall beneath fatal bullets, representing the end of established religion in the world. "When, after the attempted assassination on 13 May 1981, the Holy Father had the text of the third part of the Secret brought to him, wasn't it inevitable that he should see his own fate in it?" Cardinal Ratzinger asked. "When the Mother's hand deflected the fateful bullet, we were shown once again that there is no fixed destiny, that faith and prayer can influence history and that in the end prayer is more powerful than bullets and faith more powerful than armies."

For the more than 300 journalists in the Sala Stampa and the millions who watched the Vatican's press conference on TV, the event of the year was rather disappointing. Expectations were too high. We hoped we could look behind the veil of time and see our inescapable fate. Nothing like that was revealed.

The authenticity of the text was questioned. There was disappointment from those who expected the date for doomsday, the return of Christ, or at least, a harsh condemnation of the modern Church. But only a handful of people knew the contents before May 31, 2000, and all the speculations were based on rumors and a few short, cryptic comments by insiders.

When the Secret was revealed in the presence of Sister Lúcia, there was no indication that she disagreed with it. None of the comments she gave to the media afterwards, which were presented mostly on Portuguese television, gave any indication that this was not the true Third Secret. On the contrary, she looked relieved that the secret was finally out.

Skeptics requested the publication of Lúcia's handwritten notes. In its wisdom, the Vatican released a facsimile of her handwriting, together with several examples of letters that she had written by hand three years ago. These were taken from her memoirs, which have been available to the public for many years, so there could be no doubt that the handwriting was genuine. A professional graphologist confirmed this by comparing the Secret to one of the journals she wrote during the same year, 1941.

But didn't Bishop Venancio state that the Third Secret was written in twenty-five lines, when the Vatican has now published a text that is fifty-nine lines long? Actually, the bishop might have been mistaken, since he saw the paper through a closed envelope. It turns out that the authentic text was written on both sides of two pieces of small notebook paper with sixteen lines on each sheet. Together, they would be the same size as a folded piece of copy-book paper with twenty-five lines.

The Vatican's interpretation of the text was also criticized. In an immediate press release from the renegade Canadian priest Father Nicholas Gruner, he accused the Vatican of "whitewashing" and "watering down" the message. "The official interpretation raises far more questions than it answers," he stated.

I decided to spend the following week in Rome, speaking to several Vatican sources and doing a long interview with Archbishop Bertone, to find the answers to these questions.

One of the most frequently cited problems is that the official text of the Third Secret does not correspond to the "diplomatic version" which has circulated since 1963. As we know, even the originator of that version, the Swiss journalist Louis Emrich, admitted that it was constructed on rumors and information he received from the Vatican and that it was not meant to be the original text.

Interestingly, we find that the part of it that mentions "fire falling from the heavens," interpreted as the danger of nuclear war, is present in the authentic text. It is possible that Emrich's source indeed came from Rome, but that the truth became buried under a burden of assumptions, interpretations, rumors, and wrong conclusions.

Archbishop Bertone's research has not revealed any evidence of a Vatican leak, or for Emrich's claim that the Secret was shown to Krushchev or Kennedy. Still, it is possible that the Vatican peace initiative was influenced by the Fatima message.

The Third Secret also does not correspond to what Pope John Paul II allegedly said about it in Germany in November 1980. But this statement, ". . . when one reads that the oceans will flood entire portions of land, that human beings will die within minutes, and in millions. . . ," quoted by the German Catholic publication *Stimme des Glaubens* (Voice of Faith) was never officially verified.

Also, we now know that he did not read the authentic Third Secret before July 1981. Therefore, even if the quote is accurate, he could have only have been referring to the "diplomatic version," which he surely read in Monsignor Corrado Balducci's article "Profezia e Realta" in the *Osservatore della Domenica* the day before his election to the papacy in October 1978.

We have been told that the Third Secret had to start

with the words, "In Portugal, the dogma of the faith will always be preserved," the line Sister Lúcia quoted in her fourth memoir. But these words are now assumed to be the last line of the Second Secret which had already been revealed, announcing the spread of Communism and the persecutions of the Church. Indeed, Portugal was spared both, as we already know.

Why did Sister Lúcia state that the Third Secret should be published after 1960 when it "could be understood better"? This is still a mystery that even Archbishop Bertone does not understand. When he asked her in April 2000, she simply replied, "It was not Our Lady, I fixed the date, because I had the intuition that before 1960 it would not be understood, but that only later it would be understood." It has been speculated that this date indicates a connection with either a nuclear threat or the Second Vatican Council.

Why was it kept secret for eight decades? In order to address this, you must imagine for a moment that you are the pope. You have the burden of responsibility for the Church, its two thousand years of history, the faith of one billion people on Earth. How would you react if you read this horrific scenario? Pope John XXIII trembled. He did not want to spread fear; he wanted a state of optimism in the church in preparation for the upcoming Council. Pope Paul VI, who read the text on March 27, 1965, followed this decision.

John Paul II wanted to wait until the situation calmed down. After all, the Secret showed the death of a pope under gunfire. This could have referred to a second attempt on his life. His enemies could misunderstand the vision and see it not as a warning but as a prediction of their final victory over the Church.

When the Soviet Union collapsed, it was far from clear that Communism had finally been defeated. It was originally decided to publish the Third Secret after the death of Sister Lúcia. But while considering his upcoming trip to Portugal for the beatification of Jacinta and Francisco, the pope felt that the time to release it had finally come.

Does the Third Secret really refer only to the past? Cardinal Ratzinger insisted that, "insofar as individual events are described, they belong to the past."

Cardinal Sodano, during his speech in Fatima on May 13, 2000, was careful to say that those events "now seem part of the past." Today, Sister Lúcia seems to agree with this interpretation. But when she wrote to the pope on May 12, 1982, she stated, "And if we have not yet seen the complete fulfillment of the final part of this prophecy, we are going towards it . . . with great strides." That was one year *after* the assassination attempt. Her statement remains confusing.

One thing that reinforces my belief that the text that was revealed was the real one is the fact that the image of a pope walking over the corpses of dead priests, bishops, and religious people is not found in the Fatima Secret alone. It is a common theme in Christian apocalyptic prophecy, and appears in several revelations.

Abbess Maria Steiner, who died in 1862, wrote, "I see the Lord as he will be scourging the world and chastising it in a fearful manner, so that few men and women will remain. The monks will have to leave their monasteries and the nuns will be driven out of their convents, especially in Italy . . . The Holy Church will be persecuted . . . Unless people obtain pardon through their prayers, the time will come when they will see the sword and death, and Rome will be without a shepherd."

In May 1873, Saint Don Bosco, one of the greatest saints of the nineteenth century and founder of the order of the Salesian fathers, had a vision. "It was a dark night, the people were unable to discern which way to take to return to their homes, when in the heavens a magnificent light appeared, illuminating the paths of the wanderers as if it was midday. In this moment, a crowd of men, women, old people, children, monks, nuns, and priests, headed by the pope, came out of the Vatican and formed a procession. But behold, there came a violent storm. It darkened the light and a battle between the light and the darkness seemed to develop. Meanwhile, I saw a square covered with corpses and wounded people. . . ."

Should we now conclude that we no longer have to pay attention to predictions which point to the assassination of a pope, since the killing of Pope John Paul II was miraculously prevented? According to Saint Malachy, whose prophetic list of future popes was

quoted earlier, the greatest persecution of the Church
did not happen during the twentieth century, but will
take place during the reign of the next-to-last pope.
Malachy predicted "the last extreme persecution of the
Holy Roman Church." During that time, Pope Peter II
"will guide his sheep" through many tribulations, and
"when these have passed, the City of Seven Hills
[Rome] will be destroyed and the terrible Judge will
pass judgment over His people." Is this the future of
mankind? If we listen to the message of Fatima, we
know that it is up to us.

The rise of Communism could not have been fore-
seen by three illiterate Portuguese peasant children, and
its sudden fall came as a surprise to all of us. It is astonishing how correctly, even in the details, the Second
Secret predicted events of the twentieth century. This indicates that there is a supernatural power directly inter-
vening in human history.

Still, mankind has free will, the right to make decisions about our future. Fatima gave us the message that
it is possible to change the future by altering the
chain of cause and effect, through prayer and conversion, and by rituals like the consecration of the world to
Mary.

It was no coincidence that Fatima happened in 1917,
a year more full of tragic consequences than any other in
the last century. It was part of an emergency plan for
mankind.

"The action of God, and the equal responsibility of

man in the drama of his freedom, are the two pillars upon which history is built," Archbishop Bertone concluded in his talk with me. "Our Lady, who appeared at Fatima, reminds us that we are active and responsible partners with God in creating our future."

ABOUT THE AUTHORS

MICHAEL HESEMANN studied History and Cultural Anthropology at Gottingen University, Germany. He is an internationally respected expert on Frontier Sciences and member of the Society for Scientific Exploration (SSE). Since 1984, he has published *Magazine 2000,* Europe's largest publication on paranormal phenomena. Hesemann's books, including *The Cosmic Connection* and *Beyond Roswell,* are international bestsellers, which were published in 14 countries, including the US and UK.

WHITLEY STRIEBER is the author of *Communion* and such novels as *The Wolfen, The Hunger,* and the award-winning children's book *Wolf of Shadows*. He is co-author of the best-selling *The Coming Global Superstorm*. Mr. Strieber was born and raised in Texas.